Guidance from the Other Side

First published 2025

Copyright © Julie Ann Tyso 2025

The right of Julie Ann Tyso to be identified as the author of this work has been asserted in accordance with the Copyright, Designs & Patents Act 1988.

All rights reserved. No part of this book may be reproduced, stored in a retrieval system, or transmitted in any form or by any means, digital, electronic, electrostatic, magnetic tape, mechanical, photocopying, recording or otherwise, without the written permission of the copyright holder.

The intent of the author is to only offer information of a general nature to help you in your quest for emotional and spiritual wellbeing. Any use of the information in this book, either directly or indirectly, is at the reader's discretion and risk. Neither the author nor the publisher can be held responsible for any loss, claim or damage arising out of the use or misuse of the suggestions made, the failure to take medical advice or for any material on third party websites.
If you are struggling with any of the issues raised in this book, please contact an appropriate registered charity, such as: Cruse Bereavement Support (www.cruse.org.uk) or Samaritans (www.samaritans.org).

Published under licence by Brown Dog Books and
The Self-Publishing Partnership Ltd, 10b Greenway Farm, Bath Rd, Wick, nr. Bath BS30 5RL, UK

www.selfpublishingpartnership.co.uk

ISBN printed book: 978-1-83952-941-2
ISBN e-book: 978-1-83952-942-9

Cover design by Andrew Prescott
Internal design by Andrew Easton

Printed and bound in the UK

This book is printed on FSC® certified paper

Guidance from the Other Side

Julie Ann Tyso

By the same author:

Answers from the Other Side Published in the UK by Brown Dog Books.
ISBN 978-1-83952-487-5

Dedication and Acknowledgements

This book is dedicated to everyone who wants to know more about why we are here on earth at this time and how we can feel a closer connection to the spirit world whilst in a physical body. If you have ever thought "Surely, there must be more than this?", or felt that the spirit world might already be trying to help you through dreams, messages or even by imparting feelings, then this book has been written for you.

The information within has been designed to enhance the connection that we all have to a source greater than ourselves. It attempts to provide practical ways to benefit from the guidance on offer, to grow your soul connection and to feel more in control of your life.

What is within these pages is the result of a lifelong learning quest to find an answer to how we can make the most of our time here. Some of the information has been channelled directly from several spirit beings and some has been consolidated from literally hundreds of messages received from the spirit world, and then added to understanding gained from reading, research and teaching over many years.

So many souls, on both sides of life, have assisted me with this book. There are far too many to mention here, but whether it was the result of a chance meeting or whether I speak to you every day, please know that I could not have done any of this without you.

With love …

Contents

Preface	11
INTRODUCTION	13
CHAPTER 1: IDENTIFYING YOUR TRUE SPIRITUAL ESSENCE	17
What does it mean to be spiritual in the 21st century?	17
Mediums and Psychics	21
Soul Progression	24
Identifying Your True Essence	25
Methods of Connection	29
Connection Tools	30
Tarot and Oracle Cards	30
Dowsing	31
Crystals	31
Other Methods	32
Where do I start?	34
Strengthening the Connection	36
Writing a Journal	37
Chapter 1: SUMMARY	42
CHAPTER 2: ESTABLISHING A CLEAR VISION	44
Deciding What's Important	44
In Pursuit of Happiness	47
Recording What Makes You Happy	51
Feeling the Guilt	55
Having a Clear Vision	57
Why you need one	57
Deciding What Your Vision Should Be	61
Loving who you are	61
Decide the Life You Want	64
Relationships	64
Career/Job	65
Family	67
Finances	69

Social Activity	70
Be Careful What You Wish For	71
Sabotaging the Vision, and How Not To	73
Chapter 2 Summary: Establishing a Clear Vision	77
CHAPTER 3: HARNESSING INNER GUIDANCE	78
The Concept of Enough	78
Clearing Space	79
The Process of Clearing Space	81
Why We Hold On To Stuff	83
Categories of Clutter	86
Work Items	86
Books and Magazines	88
Clothing	89
Sentimental Items	92
Useful Someday	93
Making Decisions	95
People	97
After the Decluttering	99
Uplifting Your Home	100
Feng Shui	100
Home Energy Flow	101
Maintenance	105
The Body as a Sacred Space	106
Food	106
Movement	110
Working With Inner Guidance – Looking for the Signposts	111
Seeing the Signs	112
Coincidences	119
Listening to Your Dreams	122
False Signs	123
Chapter 3 Summary: Harnessing Inner Guidance	125
CHAPTER 4: OVERCOMING BARRIERS TO PROGRESS	127
Identifying Your Barriers To Success	128
Energy Exchanges	133
How the Exchange Appears To Work	134

Control Drama Groups	136
The Poor Me	137
The Aloof	138
The Interrogator	139
The Intimidator	140
Everyday Dealings With the People We Love	142
Dealing With the Doubters	145
Self-Sabotage	150
Chapter 4 Summary: Overcoming Barriers to Progress	152
CHAPTER 5: STEPPING INTO YOUR TRUE POWER	153
Walking in Nature	153
Moving Gracefully	159
The Ten Lessons	161
We Are All Work In Progress	170
Using Our Power To Help and Heal Others	172
Remote Healing	173
A Strategy For Moving Forward	174
CHAPTER 5 SUMMARY: Stepping Into Your True Power	176
PRACTICE RESOURCES	178
A: Meditation To Connect To Your Soul Self	178
B: Journaling Exercise	180
C: Gratitude Exercise	182
D: Happy Balance Wheel	183
E: Recording Your Vision	186
F: Self-Sabotage Exercise	189
G: Dream Template	191
I: Strategy Template	192
A SINCERE "THANK YOU"	193
REFERENCES	194
BIBLIOGRAPHY	195

Preface

There is more to life than this. Do not doubt it for a millisecond! You know it and you can feel it. At least you can feel it if you learn to quieten the noise that we call "life" and listen, really listen to your own internal, soul-inspired, guidance mechanism.

What follows is the result of channelled conversations, much reading and quite honestly having far too many questions for which answers were demanded. As with all books of this nature, it is important that the information presented here passes through your own filter: does it "feel" right to you? If not, discard it for now and pick the book up where you left off at some later date. At that point you may be surprised how relevant the next section is, or that you are now ready to accept the information in a way that you were not before. The spirit world works on many levels and in many different ways with all of us. This book is about **you** and how the words contained within might help **you**. The aim is to leave you inspired, more at peace and comforted in the understanding and control that you now have in your life.

You can read this book in the traditional way from front to back, cover to cover, or you can dip in and out. You can put it down for weeks, months or even years if you want to, but please keep it close by. This is about remembering who you are and that will be easier on some occasions than others. After each chapter there is a summary so that you can make sure you haven't missed anything. Not every chapter will be relevant to you, and may not represent your current challenges. If that is the case, then skip that bit altogether or come back to it when it seems more appropriate. The chapter summary will help you to find the relevant section when you go back.

This isn't a sprint or a marathon. It is about getting to know someone – you – and that can take hours or years, but it is well worth the effort.

GUIDANCE FROM THE OTHER SIDE

By making this connection to your spiritual self, you are reinforcing your connection to the divine. It will help you to step back and look at life in new and exciting ways. By reconnecting with your immense power, you will grow in confidence and see a clear pattern running through your life that enables you to reach your full potential and to be in the best position possible to help others. It is an exciting journey and it starts here.

INTRODUCTION

The key to understanding how the universe works, is to accept that we are all spiritual beings first and foremost. We are not physical beings who happen to have a spirit body – we are spiritual beings who all derived from the same one source and who will eventually return to that same source. We do, for now at least, have a consciousness that feels "individual" to us; what we might recognise as our personality. That personality consciousness survives our physical death. Yes, it is true, and it applies to everyone whether people choose to believe it or not.

These concepts can be a great deal for many people to take in. If you have picked up this book, you are presumably at least open to the idea. Life after death is not just a nice fuzzy possibility, it is a fact of life. On a daily basis, Mediums from all over the globe are connecting with people in spirit and passing messages on to loved ones on this side of life. Admittedly some Mediums are better than others, some messages are clearer than others, but the evidence that is brought through often provides clear proof that physical death is not the end. Our spirit friends and relations watch over us from another realm and the love that they felt for us does not die with them; neither should our love for them.

So all this begs the question: why are we here? If there is a life beyond this one that is by implication better, why are we living on this Earth with all its catastrophic so-called "acts of God", man-made wars and immense human suffering for so many people, when we could have just stayed where we were? Well, that is a very good question and the answer is "to experience".

We are incarnated in physical form because we cannot achieve the polar extremes of experience in the spirit world. It is only by experiencing the opposite of what you want and need that you recognise and appreciate what will truly make you complete. In the spirit world those polar opposites are not so easy to achieve. It is only by being born that we can fully grow our soul spirit body and progress our understanding. Our physical bodies are just coats that we put on to protect us on our journey through life. They are not "us" and although they may represent some aspect of our spirit body, they certainly are not it. All that happens at death is that we shed a coat that is no longer fit for purpose and we continue the progression elsewhere.

You might wonder why all this learning and progression of the soul is so important. My understanding from information that was given to me in a book that predates this one and was channelled from a spirit called Battrick, is that we are part of something much bigger. We are connected to everything that ever was and ever will be, and it is mutually beneficial for our soul to progress. The ultimate aim is for every soul to achieve a "bliss state" where we communicate telepathically and all our interactions are those of love. It would be very easy to scoff at that last sentence, but what choice do we have? From where I am sitting, a bliss state seems far preferable to anything we are experiencing now.

So how do we get from here to bliss? I believe that the answer is to "live the spirit within". We need to find that spirit body hidden away in the very dense physical one and "be spiritual" in all dealings. We need to make friends with the spiritual part of ourselves and recognise that spiritual soul guidance which will make our lives here easier and more tolerable. So how do we do that? How do we find a way to live the spirit within? What does it even mean to be spiritual in the 21st century?

My belief is that it is a lot easier than it sounds! Which is my reason for writing this book. Does it mean that we must denounce all material things, wear long flowing robes, carry crystals, go to live under canvas in a forest and only eat plants? Does it mean that we must practise yoga every morning and never drink alcohol? And does it mean that if we do all those things, we will eventually become "perfect" souls? As admirable as some of those things are, everyone can live a spiritual life if they choose to do so without having to do any of those things. In fact, we cannot avoid "being spiritual" because we have a spirit body as well as a physical one. All we need to do is to remember who we truly are. We need to live in the knowledge that we are all from the same source and will eventually return to that source after many lifetimes and after inhabiting many different physical bodies. Being spiritual means that we accept and understand that the true essence of who we are cannot die with our physical body. It also means that we treat and respect others as though they are part of us – which in fact, they are.

Living the spirit within means that we need to wake up to these facts – and fast. We can no longer allow ourselves to feel separate from others, wherever they reside. When we find the spirit within, we become reacquainted with our personal guidance mechanism. We learn to tap into our wisdom and the wisdom contained in every cell of the universe. We are all spiritual beings having a physical experience, but the energy on earth is so dense and often negative that it surrounds us with a fog that separates us from our true power. This book will give you the tools to remember your true spiritual essence and help you to live a more spiritual life on earth.

This isn't about being perfect. This isn't about giving up everything you own, or all the things you love. Our spirit body wants us to be happy, fulfilled and loved. This isn't about saying that you must never get cross or feel frustrated with life. It is acknowledging that living on earth has many challenges, but by remembering who you really are you can look at those problems differently and progress your soul's development.

The time to act is now. There needs to be a tipping point for the world to change. Developed societies in the Western world have more than they have ever had in material terms and yet so many people are unhappy. There is enough for everyone but, as we know, not everyone has enough. There are people inflicting horrific harm on others in name of their chosen cause. The world feels a very frightening place for many who lack freedom and fear abuse. How can this possibly be the case at this point in our earthly development? We can change the world and we can do it by changing ourselves, one soul at a time.

To get your soul a little bit closer to that bliss state you start by remembering that you have a spirit body and that is your true essence. Your soul is who you are – you are not just flesh and bone which cease to exist after death, your spirit body is the consciousness that continues to exist; it always has and always will. It can guide you and help you on your life's journey if you can just learn to listen to it. You have forgotten to look for it because you have forgotten that it exists. This book takes you on a journey to reconnect with your spirit body so that you can tap into its power – your power.

CHAPTER 1
IDENTIFYING YOUR TRUE SPIRITUAL ESSENCE

What does it mean to be spiritual in the 21st century?

We have a physical body that we are fairly well acquainted with. We know roughly how it works and we know that if we abuse it then there will eventually be repercussions in some form or another. Sometimes we know the consequences of putting undue strain on our physical form and often decide to do what we want anyway, either because we feel we have no choice or because we feel we will get away with it. Either way, we have a reasonable idea where we stand.

The spirit body however is less well known to us. Many people deny its very existence, believing that the physical body is all there is. The truth of the matter is, our spirit body is the true essence of who we really are. The physical body is who we are pretending to be and we have made such a good job of it that we have forgotten who and what we really are.

We have been following a cycle of birth and death for so long that we feel connected to the world's imperfections and restrictions. We have now reached a point where we know no better. We make the same mistakes lifetime after lifetime, and in doing so, we get further away from our source – the reason we are here in the first place. We have also become oblivious to our power.

If we take time to remember now who we are, we approach all stages of our life and death with greater patience and understanding. By knowing ourselves we can understand and help others. We reconnect with the true essence of our soul and regain our power.

GUIDANCE FROM THE OTHER SIDE

Rather than being buffeted around like a small boat on an unpredictable and often stormy ocean, we start to recognise the winds which drive us and we then have more control over the direction we wish to take. As spiritual beings having an earthly experience, we cannot completely live as we would in the spirit world because we are bound by the physical constraints of our planet. But we can reconnect with our soul and bring an understanding into our lives, which has been hitherto unknown to us. With understanding comes knowledge and then we have more control of our destiny, especially how we react to things that happen to us. Rather than bobbing around on the ocean we learn how to set a course and direct our sails to catch the wind. We realise what is important and where we want to go, and what we want to do when we get there.

We are not our bodies! They are just those coats that we have chosen to wear. We are neither male nor female, old nor young, thin nor fat, nor any other polar opposites you can think of. We are pure energy and that energy reflects our thoughts and deeds. The problem is, most of us have forgotten that!

We don't have to wait, and certainly should not wait until after death to be reconnected with our spiritual self. We can do it now, today, tomorrow and for the rest of our earthly lives. We can learn to listen to that wise inner voice that seems to know in what direction to travel, and what to do when we get there. We can see love and beauty in everything around us. In short, we see the bigger picture and how events play out in our earthly lives, and then we can regain our power.

You may ask, "Why now?". Well, the spirit world and especially our soul bodies want to finally end the separation between us. They want us to work together for the benefit of everyone and move towards that bliss state on Earth. We have been cast adrift for too long and it has not helped our personal development or the health of our planet. The time to come together is now, so that we move forward during this critical time in our history to a place of greater understanding and acceptance. We need to know and acknowledge that 'we are all one'. We are all made of the same energy as everyone and everything else. We are part of nature and not just in it. We also need to recognise once and for all that our consciousness, the true essence of who we are, continues to exist after death. Death is most definitely not the end. It is a staging point on our journey home – just that.

I do appreciate that this can be a lot to take in. A belief in the afterlife gives you the chance to dip in or out of the concept when the full reality of it bites. To really know that there is an afterlife is a total acceptance of you and your place in the universe. It challenges much of what you may have held dear. If our loved ones die, where do they go? Can they see us? Can we find a way to see them? Accepting that a consciousness, our soul, survives mortal death can be hard to accept in anything other than a hypothetical way, but it is anything but hypothetical. It is real. It happens to everyone and it isn't the least bit scary. Our consciousness is probably best described as being "non-local" to the physical body. That is to say that although associated with it, consciousness whilst living in a physical form is not entirely encased within the body. It can travel. This can be through our thoughts, dreams or in meditation.

As the coat that is our physical body is discarded, our spiritual body (our consciousness) is set free to continue its life in purely spiritual form. And live it does! This isn't something vague and fluffy that is happening – it is very real and some souls who pass quickly may not immediately be aware that things have changed.

What we first experience when we pass to the spirit world depends largely on what our preconceived ideas or religious background have programmed us to expect. A point to make here is that there is no hell. Other than the hell experience that we design for ourselves. If we pass to the spirit world feeling guilty and ashamed for acts we have carried out then we may create a "hell experience" as that is what we are expecting. We are not being judged by anyone else, only ourselves, so anyone expecting recriminations or accolades may be surprised. That is not to say that we can do just as we please on earth without consequences – quite the opposite. We have a personal responsibility and the way we live our lives on earth is held within our soul and is reflected in the level of vibration of each soul body.

If we have been engaged in criminal, cruel or murderous activities here on earth, then they will have the effect of lowering our soul's vibrational energy. If we always put ourselves before others and have a blatant disregard for the well-being of other people and the planet, then how can we expect to progress to the higher echelons of the spirit world? Regardless of celebrity or financial status, which exalt people's standing in this world, the spirit world sees things as they really are and unkind words, or even thoughts, can have the effect of lowering our vibration. Motivation is everything. We have all said or done the wrong thing and unintentionally hurt others, but if our intentions were pure and for the best then of course we take that into account when judging ourselves, because judge ourselves we do. In the spirit world there is nowhere to hide.

My understanding is that the level of soul vibration is the determining factor in where we reside in the spirit world. There appear to be many layers and although there is no hell, lower-energy vibrational souls which have lived a life that has caused pain and suffering to others will be on a lower-level plane than someone who tirelessly worked for the good of humankind. Most of us will fall somewhere in the middle of these extremes and it would appear that progression is everything!

What actually happens when we pass from this world into the next is covered in my first book called *Answers from the Other Side*. That work was the result of a question and answer session with a sprit called "Battrick" that took place over several months. Although a Medium, and someone who had done a fair amount of reading, I still didn't have a clear answer as to what actually happens when we die, and on hearing my questions, the spirit world gave me the wonderful opportunity to channel the words of an evolved spirit who was prepared to spend time with me to give me the information I craved. Essentially, at the first stage and after a period of adjustment, departed souls settle into whatever level is appropriate and "live". They have the opportunity to do many of the things that they enjoyed on earth and to look in on loved ones still living on earth. To communicate with people on this physical plane, they need to lower their vibration and people here need to raise theirs. This can be quite daunting for most people without any sort of training, and this is where Mediums come in to help. We provide the middle point that acts as a bridge between the two worlds.

Mediums and Psychics
It is appropriate here to clarify the distinction between a Medium and a Psychic. A Medium will have psychic ability as well, but mainly uses their abilities to raise their energetic vibration and enable them to talk to people who have passed to the spirit world. They recount what they are being told (either through a form of telepathy, or sometimes heard words), what they see (possibly in form of a mind's eye picture and sometimes via physical sight), and/or what they sense. Most Mediums that I know use a combination of all three things and are best described as being "clairsentient". Mediums should ideally be able to give you information about a loved one in spirit that provides you with clear evidence of the continuation of the consciousness of that person in the spirit world. This could be information about the life that they lived when they were here, shared memories, and ideally actual names and descriptions of places that are known to the recipient. The latter can be quite difficult to achieve but certainly should be the aim of all working Mediums. Sometimes the message contains evidence to suggest that the spirit person is aware of things which have happened since they passed into the spirit world; the birth of a baby, for example, or someone who has passed examinations. The aim of

the Medium is to faithfully recount what they have been told, but as the information given to us can come in multiple forms, some interpretation is necessary. It is this interpretation that can potentially throw a reading off-course. There are excellent Mediums around who have worked very hard to minimise any misinterpretation in their readings and stay connected to the spirit person so that they can feel their energy, emotions and true essence. When presented with an image and a feeling, for example, it is all too easy for the Medium to make assumptions about what those images and feelings mean, based on their personal experience, and that may not be what was intended by the spirit messenger. The spirit world uses what is in that Medium's database and sometimes lines can get crossed. Speaking from my own experience, connecting as a Medium requires a soul-to-soul blending with the spirit communicator and, I believe, considerable training to fully understand the diverse and wonderful ways that the spirit world use to communicate with us. We owe it to the people who ask us to read for them to provide the clearest evidence possible, so that the recipient is left in absolutely no doubt that they have had a conversation with their loved one in spirit. Furthermore, it may be the only opportunity that the spirit person has to communicate something that is important to them. I would love to say that every single reading that I do is a perfect version of the above; suffice to say that some go much better than others! I would however like to acknowledge the excellent tutorship that I have been so fortunate to receive from my teacher, Mr Paul Jacobs of the Arthur Findlay College. In his pursuit of excellence, he encourages all his students to be the best that they can possibly be. The style of mediumship that I adopt today is based solely on his teaching.

Some Mediums use their spirit guides and the spirit guides of their recipients to provide guidance, rather than just connecting to people who have shared a life with the sitter on Earth. Whatever the approach, Mediums usually do not predict the future and certainly do not tell you what you should do. They will however pass on messages that may include suggestions or encouragement from the spirit world if that is what they have been told. It is important to note that you should never approach any sort of reading expecting anyone else to make any decisions for you. You may have trusted the opinion of a person when they were here and desired their approval, but all decisions are yours and yours alone. Your soul progression demands that you exercise your own free will.

The job of a Psychic is to read energy or the aura of the person/subject sitting opposite them. They will almost certainly use the same clairsentient methods as Mediums but do not claim to be having a direct conversation with a person in spirit. The guidance and information that they provide can be most valuable and many will use additional divination techniques such as tarot cards or any other tools that they are comfortable using. Whether you visit a Psychic or a Medium (and many of us are both), it is extremely important that you don't leave your common sense and personal responsibility at the door! If you are told something in a reading, see how it feels to you. Does the information you have been given make sense, given what else you know? Make sure that you are not reading more into the information than was given to you, or drawing expanded conclusions about what you should do next. If a Psychic tells you that they see you moving to larger house, it does not make sense on any level to go home and immediately call an estate agent! Especially when you know that your company has been losing money and economic indicators say that this is a terrible time to move house. Just add the information that you have been given into the mix and put everything in context. Sometimes we get things wrong, but in any case, a psychic reading is just a snapshot in time of one of the many possibilities that might happen to you. We all have free will and what I am suggesting is that you learn to build up a relationship with your own soul and develop your own guidance.

Soul Progression

If we accept that the spirit world consists of several layers vibrating at different frequencies, then we can think about soul progression in terms of raising our soul's vibration to a higher frequency. We need to remember that we do not have to wait until death to do this – we can progress the soul prior to that. When we leave this physical world, we still have soul progress to make but the more we connect to our soul body while we are here, the greater understanding we take with us. More than that, by fully knowing who we truly are, we move forward in a more purposeful way. We know that when we help others, we are also helping ourselves. When we send out healing, we are healing ourselves. If we fully accept that we are all equal and we are all one then if we allow injustice, we are injuring ourselves. If we encourage poverty, we are making ourselves poor, and when we witness violent acts, we are allowing that violence into our own lives. We cannot individually change the world, but we can change how we view the world and our reaction to the things that happen in it. If we make a connection to our true essence, then we start to see the bigger picture forming in our lives. By making that connection we regain our power, so that we can be the change that needs to happen; not only to ourselves but to everyone. We change the world one soul at a time.

If looking for further incentive, my understanding is that souls on a higher plane are able to travel down to a lower one but I am not sure (I doubt, in fact) that this is true in reverse. Why would higher-level planes with evolved souls wish to live with lower-frequency souls who still have a great deal to learn? However, I know that higher-level souls return to earth frequently to impart information and aim to help us, so that implies that they have that mobility. One thing that we do know is that "like attracts like". Which could account for how these levels are formed in the spirit world.

It is my intention that this should be a "how to" guide, and with so much about the spirit world being taken on trust or in faith, it is essential to provide the practical steps needed to harness all the help available. Building a relationship with your spirit body is not an arduous task but it does require some dedication.

Identifying Your True Essence

When we say that we are going off to "find ourselves", we seem to envisage that our true selves will be discovered on a dusty path, maybe halfway up a mountain, in some remote exotic location. At that point we will have passed through several countries, filled our bags with dream catchers and religious icons and visited more monasteries and churches than we can remember. But why would we find ourselves there? What does "finding yourself" even actually mean? If you are looking for the more spiritual "you" then you don't need to go far at all.

When we talk about our soul or our true essence, we tend to think about it in an abstract and cloudy way. Our "soul" leaves our body after death, our "soul" lives on in a place we may refer to as Heaven. When we think about it, "soul" and "sole" are pronounced the same. They are singular and they have an individuality about them; they belong to us and we perceive that essence as being individual to us. It isn't halfway up a mountain (unless that is where we are); it is with us (within us) all the time.

A very long time ago, before we incarnated in any lifetime, that individual energy was part of something much bigger. At some point, that thing which we now describe as our soul was part of one source. My soul, your soul and the soul body of every living thing on earth and in other realms originated from the same place. It cannot be any other way. We are absolutely all made from the same stuff which makes all the discontent and awful acts done in the world in the name of distinctions between religious creed, physical appearance, sexual orientation or birth location (or any other "difference" someone wishes to perceive), all the more unbelievable. It is my belief that there is one great power source from which we all originate. This source has no gender or any other traits that would enable it to be personified. It just is. But I do believe that it has the ability to expand and it does that by absorbing, or maybe downloading knowledge from the individual souls it gave rise to. I don't have the brain capacity to begin to explain in scientific terms what might be going on but what I have read and have been told in a spiritual sense leads me to this conclusion. The reason we are here on earth is to experience the many extremes and dimensions of life, and as part of something larger and more powerful, in doing so we contribute to a universal knowledge.

So we all have our part to play. Our soul body that we have a duty to progress is connected to other soul bodies and the highest, most powerful source. I honestly believe that the differences perceived and expounded by different religions and belief systems are often fundamentally saying the same thing. There are different names for the one great source, and in personification there have arisen more variations, but deep down I suspect there are fewer differences than might at first appear. I do know that we are all equal, all equally valued – in the spirit world, at least – and that we have free will that we would do well to use wisely.

If we accept this knowledge, what can we personally do to assist with this necessary soul progression? Well, the energy that you originally identified with as being "you" hasn't gone anywhere. You have just surrounded it in a physical body and for the most part, forgotten about its existence. Unfortunately, the physical energy that is your body has had the effect of encasing your soul in an almost impenetrable coating; a coating that enables you to deny its very existence. Rather than identifying with the soul, we focus on the packaging. Society encourages us to do this and we happily oblige, whether we like what we see or not. How many of us are truly happy with our body and how many years of our lives do we spend trying to change it? It is obvious that if we want to keep something safe, then we must make sure that the packaging protects the contents. We need to focus on being healthy so that we can live our lives to the fullest, respect the body and give thanks for the wonderful work that it does. In this physical world that we live in, we need to feel good about our bodies so that we can feel good about ourselves. But let's be clear here: we are not our physical body, we are so much more.

By ignoring our true essence and the soul within, we start to believe that the physical body is all that we are. We blame it for letting us down, whether we have abused it or not. We expect it to perform the same towards the end of our earthly life as it did in the beginning. In short, we don't fully respect and understand that either. Images abound of the ideal body look and there are plenty around for us to compare to see how we are measuring up. This is where our main focus appears to go: to seek out role models of roughly the same age and see whether we are fitter/fatter/thinner/better looking/ more intelligent, and so on, and so on. If we spent a fraction of the time reading about how to get the perfect spiritual body that we do focusing on our physical one, there would be no need for me to write this book.

I am no different to anyone else. I have spent far too many years of my life trying to reach a weight that I will never be able to maintain. I have gone through the highs and lows of emotion alongside the highs and lows of the weight. Eventually I had to stand back and accept that rather than metaphorically beating myself up over not fitting the stereotype, I needed just to focus on trying to be as healthy as possible so that I could do the things I wanted to do and be the person I wanted to be. We are not our bodies, but we need to respect them. For most people they do an exceptional job. There are times when they may let us down, but if we switch the focus to healthy packaging for the soul, rather than an unhelpful obsession with the perfect and traditionally beautiful body, then we find a freedom that enables us to live our lives fully.

So where do we draw the line, you might ask? We need to look after ourselves to be healthy – surely, they are the same thing? If we are slim, toned and look good then we feel good and may suffer from less disease – what is the difference? Well, there is a subtle difference and it is about degree and acceptance. We each have to draw our own line in the sand. We need to reject the traditional stereotypes that are thrown at us and recognise them for what they are. We are all truly beautiful spirit souls in our own unique way and as such, we know exactly what we need to do to look after our bodies in the best way possible. Other than for some researched additional guidance, we don't need to follow a restrictive plan that is being championed by someone else. We need to be honest and take responsibility for what we do and really connect with our inner selves to receive our own guidance about how we should live our lives in a way that will let us fulfil the plan that we have for ourselves. When you really connect to your true essence, you can see what is important. The rest is just glitz.

The soul guidance that we receive does not just apply to how we look after our physical body, of course: it covers every aspect of our life. That gut feeling we have that for some inexplicable reason something doesn't feel quite right – that can be a message from our true essence or soul. When we wake up in the morning remembering something important, or knowing we need to call someone, it could be our higher forces contacting us through sleep. But what about if we could share that guidance all the time? Well, we can. We just need to learn how to listen.

There are many words to describe what it takes to connect to your true essence and the terminology can be confusing. In addition, there are different approaches which anticipate different outcomes. For example, a trained Psychic or Medium will first look within, before throwing their energy forward or upward, in order to connect with spirit for the purpose of getting messages for other people. Someone trained in mindfulness might look within to increase the amount of calm that they have in their lives and help them deal with some of life's obstacles. In meditation we are told to "clear our minds" of extraneous thoughts so that we can concentrate on what is going on inside our body. A Yogi will talk about opening chakras and allowing chi to flow. In each case, there is a sense that we are so much more than our physical bodies. The aims vary, but the processes bear similarity.

When we sit to meditate, all we are doing is creating space. Asking someone to clear their minds of extraneous thoughts is counter intuitive and expecting technicolour visions puts most people under too much pressure. By telling ourselves that we are just giving the spirit world or our higher self the opportunity to connect with us puts things into perspective. In meditation when nothing is happening, everything is happening. The spirit world needs to explore ways to communicate with us and we are just allowing them the space to do that.

An expression that confused me for quite a while was "sitting in the power". Eventually I realised that this just meant sitting "with" the spirit world, largely without expectation that any unusual phenomena would take place. However, not understanding what was meant by this expression led me to believe that I was missing something: I was somehow deficient in something that it was important to do. When we think in terms of just creating some space or an opportunity, it makes things much easier.

For this reason, it is important that we attempt to understand how all these different methods fit together.

Methods of Connection

To recognise your spirit body within, you do not need to have any previously acknowledged psychic ability. You do not have to have seen apparitions from a young age, or "know things" from an inexplicable source. What I am suggesting is open to everyone from the youngest to the oldest. Having said that, when your connection to your own spirit is strong, you may become aware of more things and wish to develop your abilities further.

GUIDANCE FROM THE OTHER SIDE

In the first instance, this is all about guidance. About learning to feel what is right for you personally, and to take that knowledge and enrich your life. Everyone is psychic to some degree, but for many those skills are latent. Not everyone wants to develop extra sensory powers, even if they suspect they may have some. They are too busy living their lives and coping with what they have; but even those people would benefit from a stronger relationship with their spirit within.

You don't need any tools or special equipment; you already have everything you need, which is you. However, you cannot be interested in spiritual topics without coming across various tools which people use and so these are discussed briefly below.

CONNECTION TOOLS

Tarot and Oracle Cards
Some Mediums and Psychics use additional tools to help strengthen their connection to the spirit world. Originally just tarot, now there are a wide variety of cards of all types, shapes and sizes, which you can use to prompt your intuition or psychic ability. Tarot cards slightly resemble playing cards, but they contain additional images which have meanings attached to them. There is normally some sort of book included that explains the traditional interpretations, but the pictures give some clues. Often it is easier to study the meanings for a while and then just go with your gut feeling when you draw a card. People can be very superstitious around tarot cards, as though they possess some power of their own – which they do not. Some of the images can appear frightening and several have attracted negative connotations over the years, such as the Death card, which actually mostly just means that change is likely. In the right hands tarot can be powerfully accurate, but oracle cards are much softer and prettier and if you are starting out, they would be the preferred option. If

you use them just to expand your thinking and help you to view situations from different angles, they can be a very useful tool.

There are literally many hundreds of card decks printed each year; if you believe they would help, or even if you are just curious, which pack you select is purely a matter of personal preference. As with all things, you cannot leave sense and reason at the door. If you ask a question and you are emotionally invested in the answer, I do believe that it is possible to skew the outcome to what you want to see. Just as with mediumship, all outcomes are subject to different interpretation. It should also be remembered that we all have free will, so any course of action indicated can only be that "snap-shot in time"; it is important, as well, not to create a self-fulfilling prophesy and make something happen as the result of pulling a particular card.

Dowsing
Dowsing is another divination technique that is used fairly extensively. It can of course be used to find water or mineral deposits underground but we are perhaps more concerned with dowsing with a crystal or other weight on a chain to ask a specific question. Some people are extremely skilled at dowsing and get excellent results. The best Dowsers have devoted hours to this ancient craft and see it as an invaluable tool in establishing the truth. Dowsing is also used for healing and to clear energies, which is my preferred use, but these things are very much down to personal choice.

Crystals
Holding a crystal in your hand whilst connecting to the spirit world is another option and although different meanings are assigned to different types, my preference is to go with whatever you are drawn to. Clear quartz and amethyst are both lovely "all-rounders". I believe they can amplify our efforts just by being in the vicinity. I love crystals and have collected several over the years, and of course there are many books on the subject

to refer to if you want to know more. On several occasions I have been inexplicably drawn to certain crystals and end up wanting them in my life. I once drew a detailed sketch of a particular crystal I wanted and found it in a shop a couple of weeks later; the correlation between crystal and sketch was uncanny. It happens much less often now as I have quite a collection of crystals but occasionally I feel a crystal pulling me towards it and eventually I end up buying it.

Other Methods
Pretty much anything can be used as a tool to enhance psychic ability if anyone wishes to adopt it as such. Selecting one ribbon from a bowl of brightly coloured ribbons, for example, could be used psychically if required. In reality, the psychic is probably just distracting themselves in order to let their psychic ability shine through, but if it works for them then fair enough. It is fairly common at the end of the year to read that someone has attempted to predict the future by throwing sticks or even asparagus in the air to see how it lands to decide what will happen next. My view is that these things provide a bit of theatre for the people involved and are not really necessary. I have learnt, however, to keep an open mind in these matters.

It is worth mentioning here that one increasingly popular method of connecting with the spirit world is through trance mediumship. Subjects sit in some sort of enclosed space or tent and attempt to allow a spirit entity to talk through them using their voice box. The human subject or "instrument" must, in effect, "get out of the way" to allow the spirit person to speak through them. For the vast majority of people engaged in this, there is merely a light shadowing over the subject involved and they are completely aware of what is going on, but some of the best trance Mediums say that when they first sat in the chair, they appeared to fall asleep and on waking they had to be informed that someone had spoken through them.

GUIDANCE FROM THE OTHER SIDE

Some of the people most successful at this did not even claim to be psychic; one of those was Maurice Barbanell who was a journalist and wrote many books on Spiritualism. On one occasion he went into an involuntary trance to channel a spirit called Silver Birch and from then on became a channel for this spirit. Barbanell was a founding editor of *Psychic News*, established in 1932 (*Psychic News* 2023) and did not initially declare that he was the channel for Silver Birch when the works were published. The work of Maurice Barbanell and Sliver Birch has certainly provided me with some very valuable insights in trying to understand what is going on and I can thoroughly recommend these books – the details of which are included in the bibliography. There is a history of trance mediumship in the Spiritualist Church and of course it is still practised today. Whether you choose to believe in the validity or otherwise of the information brought through is entirely up to you. As with everything you read, discernment is essential. The Silver Birch books made sense to me and that is why I have included them in the bibliography, but they are by no means the only books of that type in existence and will not be the last.

All these activities are very far removed from, and I would argue superfluous to, what I am suggesting, but it can sometimes be helpful to see the bigger picture.

This book isn't about how to become a Psychic or a Medium in terms of giving readings to other people. It isn't about ghost-hunting, or capturing unusual other-worldly phenomena, so other methods are not covered in detail. This book is about your own personal connection with your spiritual self, and in doing so, your connection to the wider spirit world. Whatever approach you take, it is important to set the intention to connect only to beings of the highest vibrations and intentions. You would not open your front door and invite in anyone who happened to be passing. Therefore I strongly advise against Ouija boards, or going anywhere that you suspect might lead you to connect to anything other than higher vibrational beings. Remember that you have free will. If, in meditation or in a heightened state of awareness, something comes to you that you feel does not have your best intentions at its heart, then politely ask it to leave and call in archangels (Archangel Michael would be a good choice) and request that the unwelcome spirit be escorted away.

Where do I start?
It isn't always easy to find your own space to think. In big noisy families, space can be at a premium and having your own quiet corner, not to mention your own room, may be impossible. In an ideal world we would all have our special silent corner where we could be introspective and meditate without interruption. The reality for many people is quite different. Even if you do have your own space, surrounded by inspiring images and beautiful crystals, the space needs to be created in your head as well as in the physical world; if your head is full of other stuff then the room on its own will not help you very much. Far better, then, to go outside and walk in nature to connect with your higher self. Walking can be a meditation. Noticing the nature that is all around you is a very good start. Eventually you learn to really "see" and colours may look brighter than anything you have seen before. Sounds impossible? Try it! Learn to really see what is all around you. Look for the beauty in all things. Drink in that beauty and feed your soul.

If you can find that quiet space where you will not be interrupted, then turn your thoughts inwards and notice what you see and feel. There is a suggested meditation format in Resources (Section A). Give yourself plenty of time and work with your imagination. Just because you are imagining something doesn't make it any less effective. In fact, your imagination is incredibly powerful. So sit in your quiet space and just notice the sound of your breathing, and concentrate on that for a few minutes. If you get stray thoughts which invade your quiet space (such as, "I need to put the washing machine on and I must remember to buy some milk"), just tell yourself that you will remember those things later. Brush those thoughts away for now as best you can and get back to concentrating on your breathing.

After a few minutes, visualise a small white flame that starts somewhere near the centre of your body and gradually expands to 30 centimetres or so outside your physical body. Take it very slowly, expanding the light in your mind's eye little by little as you go. If you can't get the light to stretch that far in your imagination to start with, that's not a problem, you can work on it each time, but aim to eventually expand your light body to a little distance from your physical body. Start small and build the light slowly, using your imagination. This white light represents your aura or light-filled spirit body. Imagine that it has a thin protective shell. This special light-filled bubble is your shield or armour and has been specifically designed as a filter to let in only energy of the highest good, while still letting you send out positive energy to those who need it. See it in your imagination. You may think you are making everything up, but you have a spirit body – do not forget that. What you see in your mind's eye is no less real or relevant than things happening in the physical world. Sit surrounded in that light-filled bubble every time you connect to your soul spirit. In fact, if you are struggling with life at the moment, keep it on all day! Whenever you are met with any sort of negativity it will just bounce off the shell and not get through. When you have practised this a few times and feel really protected, you will feel liberated! Remember that when you act in kindness to others: this light-filled bubble has been designed to allow your positive energy to pass through to all who need it.

GUIDANCE FROM THE OTHER SIDE

Strengthening the Connection

When you are comfortable sitting in your light-filled bubble, and feel safe and protected, take your thoughts inwards to make that connection deep into your soul. Give yourself time. There is no rush. Try and feel the connection before you start to intellectualise it. Can you start to feel the essence of who you truly are? What does that energy essence feel like? It will be a slightly different experience for everyone. There is no right or wrong way. You are meeting, or rather reacquainting yourself with a dear old friend. There is no script to follow and no words which must be said. This is just about you being present in the moment, noticing the feelings and starting to recognise your own spiritual energy.

Take a few minutes to enjoy the feeling. Are there any words which come to you? Are there any thoughts which come into your head that might be significant? Don't be concerned if not much is happening. There is always tomorrow and the next day – things will unfold at their own pace. Eventually, though, you will start to feel or notice something. Your higher soul is very keen to have a relationship with you, too.

Because this is a personal relationship, people can approach strengthening the connection in several different ways. Some may prefer to just sit and feel enveloped in the energy and be satisfied that they know it is there. Others may desire a more verbal communication. Take your time. It is important to gain the confidence that any verbal guidance is coming from your higher self and not from your logical brain. If in doubt, go straight back to focusing on what you feel rather than what you think. Be sure, too, that any guidance will be loving and kind, and for your highest good. If you feel that this not the case then get up from your chair, walk around and make yourself a warm drink, and leave it a few days before you try again. Go outside if you can and breathe in some fresh air – feel the breeze, the wind and rain on your face, or the sun on your head. When you do have another go, spend longer checking the light-filled bubble that surrounds you. Picture it in your mind's eye, check that it completely envelopes and protects you, and only proceed if you feel comfortable in doing so. Remember that this is not a race. It is a journey, your journey, and it will be different to anyone else's.

Writing a Journal
When you regularly sit in your light-filled bubble, you will find it helpful to record anything that suddenly comes into your mind. There is something rather special about writing down your thoughts. A diary records events but a journal can record your thoughts, feelings, hopes and wishes. The process of writing often helps you to make sense of things which have happened to you in a way that just cannot not take place if you keep your thoughts in your head. The writing doesn't need to be planned, in fact it probably works best if it isn't. Just pick up a pen and start to write. You can begin by asking yourself a question, such as "Why does person X upset me?" or "Why am I feeling so anxious today?", or you can just sit there with a notebook and pen and see what happens. There is further information in Resources (Section B).

Writing a journal in this way should not be confused with automatic writing, which is when a spirit is thought to overtake your hand and write through you, and you are left to interpret the markings on the page. Writing a journal is all about your connection to your own higher spirit self. You may, however, get ideas, words, even have a conversation in your head, and you might wonder if those words are truly your own. At this stage, provided that the words are light and encouraging, it is probably best not to analyse them and just concentrate on making the connection.

If you do decide to ask a question, write that at the top of the page and sit in your light-filled bubble and see what you are inspired to write. Your soul self will have a broader view and will help you to see things from another's point of view. Go with the flow and write down anything that comes to you. If you prefer, you can sit at a laptop and type directly onto that. Whatever works best for you. In the beginning it might be easier to maintain your connection if you sit in a chair and just have some paper to hand, but it really is up to you.

When you have written in your journal, sit back and read what it says. Does the act of writing it down provide any clarity? Does it help you to see the bigger picture? Do you feel that by putting your words on a page you have unburdened yourself of some of the negative emotion that might be present? If you can't see any immediate benefit, re-read your words in a week or so and see if you feel the same way.

People often write about the most personal things and in doing so, sometimes feel vulnerable should anyone else read their words. The journal is for you – for your eyes only. It does not need to be shared unless you want it to be.

When life is hard it can be difficult to remember all the good things that we already have and an important part of living a more spiritual life is giving thanks. However bad things may appear, there is always something to be grateful for and by bringing those things to mind, we allow much more positivity to enter our lives. The gratitude can focus on things we may be tempted to take for granted: the soft bed that we sleep on, the comfortable shoes that we own. Even in our darkest moments, we can normally think of something good. In fact, during those darkest of times, that is when it is more important than ever to express our gratitude. The act of "giving thanks" is charged with positive energy. When we say thank you for what we have, we are attracting more good things to us. As far as energy is concerned, like attracts like, so when we say (or more importantly, feel) something positive, we are sending a signal out to the universe that we want more of the same. If we focus on what is missing in our lives then we attract more of the same: i.e. what is missing!

Include a section in your journal, therefore, to record all the things that are good about your life. By appreciating what we have, and especially giving thanks for it, we raise our personal energy to a higher level. It is so very easy to focus on the negative, especially when things are tough and we don't know or fear for what tomorrow might bring. When giving thanks, always focus on the present moment: thank you for the food that I have to eat today; thank you for the shelter that I have today; thank you for the support that I receive from my friend X; thank you for the flowers that I can see from my window. We can all find thanks for something, however bad things get. By bringing attention to all the good things in your life, you really do open yourself up to more good things. Negative energy is dark and heavy, and positive energy is light – pure light – and it will always rise to the surface if you give it a chance.

You can add to that gratitude section in your journal whenever you remember another good thing about your life. Remember to re-read it often. Really feel the gratitude and appreciation as you write and read the words. I cannot over-emphasise how important this is. For further information have a look at Resources (Section C).

For most of us, there is a great deal to be thankful for. Unfortunately, society has a habit of reinforcing the negative – now more than ever. We only have to read a news feed to see examples of that. As we know, news feeds are driven by "clickbait": for journalists, a measure of their success is determined by how many people click on a particular story to read an article and gain exposure to the advertising that is paying their wages. There is therefore a massive incentive for journalists to create sensational headlines. It is much easier to make a slightly negative story sound disastrous than it is to make a positive story sound wonderous. When people are worried or fearful they look for articles which reinforce their fears, rather than search for articles which allay them. It is very easy to lose perspective when you are surrounded by news that is telling you how awful the world is. As you read these articles (if you still choose to do so) it is important to recognise them for what they are.

GUIDANCE FROM THE OTHER SIDE

As with so many things, the Internet can be used for good as well as for the not so good. It is wonderful to have access to so much information, but it leaves us with the major dilemma of knowing what to believe. Absolutely anyone can produce content and some of those people have a particular agenda, and it may not be obvious, initially at least, what their particular agenda is. Even what we might call well-respected publications are not immune from negative sensationalism and bias.

So we are living in a world where we are bombarded by information every hour of the day and night, and yet it is becoming increasingly difficult to know who or what to believe. A high proportion of that information is negative and is having the effect of bringing our energy levels right down. It is more important than ever to find that personal connection with our soul and listen to its guidance. By surrounding yourself in a light-filled bubble and giving thanks and appreciation for what you have, you will bring yourself back into balance and this will eventually put you in a position where you can help others; it will help you to stay grounded.

We are spiritual beings, but we are living in a world where few acknowledge that fact and living with too much negativity can easily affect us. We are a part of this physical world and we must live in it. For most of us that means that there are bills to pay, people to feed and work to do that isn't always what we would choose. We can often feel as though we have little control over our lives and that we resemble a hamster on a wheel, or that we are on a rollercoaster that refuses to stop. Few have the luxury to sit all day and think spiritual thoughts. So we need to find a way to bring us back into balance as quickly as possible, before we spiral down into despair. We do this by controlling our thoughts and directing them to something more positive. Sometimes we have little or no control about what is happening to us, but even then we have a choice about how we react to what is happening. This is the point when we must choose something more positive.

GUIDANCE FROM THE OTHER SIDE

The gratitude list is a big part of staying positive and healthy. By aligning your energy to everything that is good, you are bringing yourself back into balance. In addition, if we can stay active and allow energy to flow through our bodies, we are giving ourselves the best possible chance to live a healthy life. I have always found the most amazing boost to my well-being if I am able to get out of the house and walk in a park or see green fields, trees and beautiful plants. The joy is almost palpable. Living life in a spiritual way involves finding joy in the simplest things, and finding joy in nature is available to almost everyone. If you can't leave the house, being surrounded by plants will help. If that isn't possible, even a picture of a natural beautiful scene may do the trick. By connecting to our soul, being grateful for everything we have and finding joy in nature, we are already starting to live more spiritually. By stretching and moving our bodies gracefully and purposefully, so that energy can flow, we are giving ourselves the best chance of feeling great, too. All these things help to ground us. We are combining mind, body and soul and they all benefit from regular focused attention.

GUIDANCE FROM THE OTHER SIDE

Chapter 1 Summary: Identify Your True Spiritual Essence
- What does it mean to be spiritual in the 21st century?
    - We are spirits which happen to have a physical body, not the other way round
    - Individual consciousness continues beyond death
    - We have chosen to be here so we can have experiences which would not have been possible if we had stayed in the spirit world
    - We never stop learning and our soul wants to progress to "a bliss state"
    - There are several layers vibrating at different frequencies in the spirit world and our soul vibration decides the level in which we reside – like attracts like
    - Understanding the difference between Mediums and Psychics
- Identifying your true essence:
    - Our individual energy was once part of a great source
    - We are still all connected and part of something much bigger
    - We need to acknowledge soul energy as distinct from the physical packaging in order to find our true essence and benefit from the guidance available
    - Explaining common terminology – just a different use of words
- Methods of connection:
    - You already have everything you need
    - There are tools which can enhance connection for some – just seeing the bigger picture (tarot and oracle cards, dowsing, crystals and other methods)
- Where do I start?
    - Find a place to think, your own quiet corner
    - Making a light-filled bubble to help you to connect

GUIDANCE FROM THE OTHER SIDE

- Strengthening the connection:
    - This is your journey, take your time, listen to the world of spirit
- Writing a journal:
    - Clarifying the process through writing
    - Recording everything you are grateful for
    - Combating negativity and returning to balance

CHAPTER 2
ESTABLISHING A CLEAR VISION

In this section we are working towards establishing what is important for the soul's development. There should be no dilemma here. What the soul wants and needs and what we want and need *should* be in alignment. Our soul wants us to be happy. We **want** to be happy! Unfortunately, a lot of people are not happy at all, or not always as happy as they could be. We carry with us a list of "shoulds" and "should nots". We have opinions about what we think is important and what can wait awhile to move up on to the important list. We often respond more readily to urgent requests (a WhatsApp message, a friend's request, a messy kitchen), rather than dealing with the important things, such as showing and telling the people we love that we care. Spending precious time with people who have precious little time left. Everyone's important list will be different, but whatever is on it, we need to be sure that we are quite clear what those things truly mean to us and not be swept along with all of life's "stuff".

Deciding What's Important
After you have spent some time in your light-filled bubble, writing in your journal and taking more walks in nature, you will reinforce the perspective that tells you what is important in your life. By spending at least a few minutes each day giving thanks for the good things, you will gain a much clearer picture about what is important to you personally. This is not so much your personal bucket list (although it could be), but more an invitation to invite into your life more of the things which are meaningful to you.

Deciding what is important is not as easy as it might sound. It may help to separate what you want and need in terms of material items and how you want to feel. For example, for some, getting an expensive smart new car might be extremely important and if you ask them what sort of car they want then they might ask for a top-of-the-range, fast convertible that will turn heads as they drive down the road. If you then ask them why they want that make and model of car, they may quote performance figures and technical data, but when you dig a bit further it is probably more about how owning that car will make them feel. It is what the car represents that is almost certainly the thing that is most important to them. If it makes them feel successful, for example, then you can delve a little further. Does owning the car represent reaching a certain point in their career? Does it represent achieving a certain level of wealth? Is it proving something to yourself, or to others, about your ability to amass sufficient wealth to buy the car? In other words, what will owning that car really mean to them? If you do not analyse the reasons why you might want something then there is a danger that the car, when you get it, is not in itself capable of making you happy.

You also have to make sure that you do not skew your view about what is important based on what other people want for you. Parents, partners and even your own children often think they know what is best for you. Often, we do not wish to challenge their opinion and may believe that they know better than we do about what is best for us. We should always respect and appreciate the advice given by friends and family and give due consideration to their suggestions if we know that they genuinely believe they are acting in our best interests; these are, however, only suggestions. The people who love us try to guide us based on their experience of life – their regrets, as well as their successes. From their life viewpoint they could be raising genuine concerns and you may be very grateful for their advice and guidance but you still need to check that what they want is best for you. By fully understanding yourself and how you want to live your life, you can make better decisions. Your parents, for example, may want you to follow in their footsteps and become lawyers and doctors, or plumbers and carpenters, because in their experience that will give you a good income and you will be able to buy a nice house, drive that smart expensive car and have a "good life". But that is their example of a good life – it may not be yours.

External influences can work against you in other ways, too. You might believe that you have an invention that could make a difference to the world, and yet your family and friends try to dissuade you. "If it is such a good idea, why hasn't someone else done it?" might be the typical response. Well, maybe it isn't a great idea, but maybe the reason it has not been done before is that genuinely no one else has thought about it, or if they did they didn't have the motivation to progress with it. No one should embark on an idea for a business without doing thorough research – it could be that the idea certainly isn't financially viable and it is much better to realise that before you start to invest in it. It is, however, better to spend time doing that research than give up before you start. Take advice from people who really understand and who are well qualified to advise you. However much we wish to live a life closely connected to spirit, we must acknowledge and respect the fact that our everyday existence is happening in the physical world. There are bills to pay and often those who rely on us for their basic needs.

When you have gone through the process and think you have identified what is important for you personally, the universe can often lend a helping hand. Your soul had a plan for you when you arrived on earth. The more you learn to connect, the more likely you are to recognise what that plan was. It isn't always a straight path and sometimes we spend time learning or working at something that seems completely alien to anything we might want to do. The fact is, from our point on earth, we do not have the bird's eye view that enables us to see the big picture, but what we do have is a feeling. We have all heard the expression "the universe works in mysterious ways" – well it does! When we are truly on track with what our soul has in mind for us, we receive encouragement. This may take the form of a book literally dropping off a bookshelf into your hands, as it has for me, or it may be an overheard snippet of conversation as you pass someone in the street. The flat you wanted so much and tried so long and so hard to buy, but eventually it fell through, only for you to find something better a few days later – this is all the universe looking out for you. We are told not to give up and to keep pushing and pushing to get what we want, but if we feel that we are hitting our heads against a proverbial brick wall, time and time again, then we need to stop and ask the question: is this really the best for me? If you understand what is important then that question is a lot easier to answer.

In Pursuit of Happiness
I am completely unqualified to be able to make any comment about depression, anxiety or any other mental or physical illness. So if you, or anyone you know is suffering, you must always refer them or yourself for professional help.

Having an illness does not, however, preclude you from acting on any of these suggestions, but they are just suggestions and if in doubt you should liaise with the professional assistance on offer and ask for their opinion first, before following any of these ideas.

Whoever you are, and regardless of any particular challenges you may or may not face, it is unrealistic to expect to be completely happy every day of your life. There will be ups and downs, and sometimes the downs can appear to go on forever. We lose people, we lose jobs, homes, pets, and sometimes even our sense of self. It is important that we acknowledge these losses and give ourselves time to grieve. After a loss we must go through a process and that will be slightly different for everyone. There are very dedicated people who will offer assistance through a number of registered bodies who will help you as much as they are able; a list of such organisations is given at the end of this book.

GUIDANCE FROM THE OTHER SIDE

For those of us lucky enough not to require professional help, happiness can be as simple as making a decision to be happy. It can be that straightforward – I didn't say that it was easy to decide to be happy, but the difference between being happy and not is often a decision to be so.

Not everyone who is poor is unhappy and not everyone who is rich is happy. It is true, however, that not being poor provides a much better environment for the happiness decision to take place. The old saying that if you are rich then at least you can be unhappy in comfort has some truth in it; it also means that you can throw money at your problems and that may solve many of them. It can't solve everything, though, and even with private healthcare or a good lawyer you can't stop people dying, or someone you love having to face something that they did wrong. Life happens. Stuff happens. Often the only freedom of choice we have is how we react to those things.

By not making the decision to be happy, we then become part of the "life stuff" that other people must deal with. Knowing that someone you love is unhappy can weigh very heavily. You desperately want to make things better for them and think, "If only I could get them a house", "If only I could get them a job/car/loving partner/new TV, etc., etc. then they would be happy". Well, you know what? They probably wouldn't be! It certainly might help in the short term as it is difficult to be happy when you feel that your life is lacking in several key elements, but that still doesn't stop you from deciding to be happy. There are people who live every day with the most awful disabilities. There are people living with a terminal diagnosis who know that they will never be able to fulfil a fraction of the things they hoped. They are not all miserable! Some are – and understandably so – but some of the most inspiring individuals are still able to learn to live with what life has thrown at them and make the best of it. If they can do that, in the most difficult of circumstances, then we should, too.

Happiness is rarely the result of acquiring something new. If you have wanted the latest "thing" and then you get it, that can give you a happiness high for a few hours, days or weeks, but you will then be looking for the next new thing to provide that high. And when you have achieved that then it will be the next, and the next, and the next, until you run out of things. Chance would be a fine thing, you might say – there will always be something you want and that is fine, but don't think that those things in themselves will make you happy in the long term. They are just not capable of it.

Happiness is much less complicated than that. You can't wait for happiness – it is too important. You must generate it now, this minute and not a second later. If you wait for a certain set of circumstances to be in place then you will miss out. You have heard the expression "fake it until you make it"? Well, that applies to happiness too. If you can't manage full-blown happiness right now, at least attempt to ditch the negative talk that accompanies unhappiness. Don't talk the unhappy talk. Don't grumble and say "If only I had this, or that"; "Things used to be better". Maybe things were better for you in the past, but how do you know what will happen in the future? The only thing I can promise is that if you always look for the negative, then that is what you will find. If you can't manage any positive words just yet then concentrate on removing negative ones from your speech. Focus on what you can do, rather than what you can't.

Looking on the positive side of life has its challenges, no one is denying that, but far better to be aligned to the positive than the negative. For the most part, people want to be surrounded by happy people, not negative ones. We all want to have a laugh, to have fun and enjoy ourselves: that is so much easier if you are in the presence of happy people. We all go through bad patches and we need our friends to help us through. We are finally learning to encourage people to talk about how they feel – really talk, especially young people – but at the same time we must cultivate our ability to listen. We need to recognise clues that people are struggling and it can be difficult to do that if we thinking about ourselves all the time, and how unhappy *we* feel. We need to recognise that not everyone can or will be happy all the time, and it certainly isn't the intention to brush unhappiness away and put on a happy front just to please others. What I am saying is that we need to start with ourselves first, to try to generate happiness from within and then spread that happiness to others through our love and friendship. Happiness is contagious! Joy and laughter are life-enhancing; why wouldn't we want to spread that around and make others happy?

When thinking about what it is important, happiness should be at the top of the list. One of the most important favours you can do for yourself is to really analyse what makes you happy. The first thing is to recognise what being truly happy feels like! It is not necessarily enjoying perfect health, having plenty of money or perfect relationships. It is not necessarily about having a well-paid job, so that you can take long and expensive holidays. It is all about the feeling: about joy, contentment and sometimes euphoria.

To feel happy, we need to feel optimistic and hopeful about the future. Depending on what has been happening to you recently, that optimism may take a knock from time to time. If you want to look forward, you need to think about what your ideal future would look like. A later section examines your vision for yourself and invites you to dare to dream! You want a future that will make you happy, so the more you understand about what makes you happy the better.

There are many reasons why people carry on doing things which make them unhappy. It is often because they cannot see any alternative to the status quo. It isn't always possible to make major changes in your life, especially when other people rely on you, but are you sure that you really have looked at all the alternatives and there is nothing else you can do? Being in the "wrong" job can make someone unhappy and a working life of probably anything up to 50+ years is far too long not to examine all possibilities. When you have a career, especially if it is one you have had to work hard to qualify for, and if it has cost you a great deal to get there, you may feel as though you can't face starting again and having to live with the drop in salary that would come with a new career, so you plod along, becoming more unhappy as the days go by. Facing your unhappiness in a job might be something that you are reluctant to do, but surely that is better than facing the next 40 or so years doing something that you hate? You can start just by analysing what would need to change in your current role for you to enjoy your job more. Earning more money is unlikely to make you love a job you hate, but it might stop you resenting the fact that others are paid more and that you feel undervalued. Reducing the workload might enable you to complete work to a better standard, which might improve job satisfaction; another option might be to reduce the commute so that you are less tired when you arrive home each night. If you can look at the problem in many different ways, you may find a solution that increases your chances of enjoying what you do.

As with all these decisions, our soul has a good idea what might be best for us and tuning in will help us to explore all the possibilities available. By taking the time to face the fear of admitting that you may have made a mistake, you are part of the way to solving it.

No one is suggesting that any of this is easy, but it might not be as impossible as you think. Life is about joy. Being joyful raises our energy and that of our soul. If you focus on joy rather than what is lacking in your life, you can raise that energy and attract more aspects of joy. It is all about what you think – about the thoughts which pass through your imagination. If you keep them positive and happy as best you can, for as long as you can, then you are lifting your whole body and soul to a high level of frequency. In short, think happy and you'll be happy!

Recording What Makes You Happy
If you have reached this part of the book, you should by now have a pretty good idea about what makes you happy and what is important to you. Now

is the time to make a few notes in your journal to record those things. Just having a vague list in your head doesn't work nearly so well. If these things are really important to you then accord them the respect of writing them down. What is important today maybe less so in a year's time and it can be useful to see how priorities change over time. In addition, the notes you make now will help when you reach the next chapter.

Achieving happiness is about balance. It is difficult to be truly happy if you have achieved success in one part of your life and not in another. For many people, having lots of money in the bank, a beautiful house and car are meaningless if there is no one to share things with. Someone else may value their freedom and genuinely prefer solitude, but may feel exhausted all the time and know that they are working far too hard. The balance will be different for everyone. The balance you need to find is the one that will make you happy. You may be sure that your soul wants you to be happy.

There are some simple techniques which will help you to achieve a happy balance in your life by identifying where improvements can be made. The Happy Balance Wheel (often just called a balance wheel) works on the basis that in order to be happy and fulfilled, you need to find a way to focus your time and attention in the areas which are most important to you. Your life will undoubtedly require pockets of time spent in very different areas, depending on what is happening for you at that moment. For example, you may be studying for an exam that will improve your career prospects and for a few weeks or months you will need to spend a greater amount of time and a large proportion of your focus on that. To devote time to passing the exam, you will need to remove your focus from other areas of your life. We can all do this from time to time with few ill effects, but over the longer term, removing our focused attention on a regular basis from important areas of our life may make us feel unhappy and as though our work/life balance has been lost. We are not always conscious of these subtle changes as they are happening, and we might not notice at all until someone points out that there is a problem. Rather than waiting until that point, finding a mechanism to alert us to potential problems can be useful. Once we have identified all the things which are important to us and which we need in place to be happy, it makes sense that we want to look after those things so that they can be the best they possibly can be.

The happy balance wheel is a visual way of ensuring that we have got the balance right. It is a technique that I have adapted from several life balance wheels which I have seen used in different contexts and one for which the origin is unclear, so unfortunately I cannot attribute this method to an original referenced source.

The aim is to create a visual representation of the happy balance that you have in your life. The idea is that the wheel represents you and there is a section representing everything that is important to you.

The first thing you must do is to draw a large circle on a piece of paper. Then divide up the circle into, say, eight sections in the same way that you might divide up a cake. Each segment of the wheel represents an area of your life that is important to you. These segments can include the roles that you play in your life: partner, parent/grandparent, student, employer/employee, friend; also your spiritual connection, your mental and physical health, and your financial freedom.

These sections are entirely personal to you and should just represent things that you care about. There can be more or fewer sections if you prefer. If you are a keen sports person then include your sport(s); you may prefer just to have a section called "family" that covers everyone you care about, rather than individual sections. There are no fixed rules as long as you manage to include everything that you truly care about.

On the outside of the wheel, against each segment, write the area of your life that it represents. Working from the centre of the circle, inside each of your segments, put a line marked 1 to 10 with 1 in the centre and 10 towards the edge.

GUIDANCE FROM THE OTHER SIDE

In Resources (Section D) you will find more information and a template that you can adapt. To complete the wheel, think about each of your marked sections and how you feel about each one. For example, if you have a section representing your significant other and you feel very happy about the relationship and you believe you have sufficient time to spend together, then you would put a cross in that section somewhere between 9 or 10 towards the outer edge. If you love sport but have not been to the gym for months and are feeling very unfit, then you might want to put a cross nearer to a one or two. You then join up the various crosses and the result will be a circle (of sorts). The nearer it is to the outer edge – especially if it is a complete circle, the greater the happy balance. There is an example of a completed template in the Resources section.

As we are all involved in a variety of different endeavours throughout our lives, we need to repeat the process every three to six months to see how we are doing; make sure you record the date whenever you do one of these. Whenever a happy balance wheel has been completed, make some notes about how you can improve the balance of happiness in your life in the areas which achieved lower scores. For example, if family has scored a low score and you know that you would love to spend more time at home, make a note of a couple of things you can start doing and some things that you can stop to help rectify the situation. When you look back on the wheel in say three months' time, you can measure your progress. If you find a section that has a low score and you find it very difficult or impossible to see how you can affect a change, then go back into your bubble and ask the question of your soul. For example, concerns about money can often affect people's ability to be truly happy. Ask the question, "What can I do to improve my financial situation?" and then really listen. Is there anything that comes to you? Do you get the feeling you should check a jobsite one more time, or go and speak to a particular person? You never know what might come up if you take the time to listen.

Your soul has a habit of speaking to you at the most unexpected times. If you focus on what is important then you are much more likely to hear what it is saying. For example, many people are looking for more love in their lives and if you are listening, you may realise that you keep hearing people talking about a particular dating website or you keep seeing advertisements for a particular group that you might join. Having said that, listening to spirit still has to be coupled with common sense! We live in a physical world. Things must be paid for and physical ability has to be considered, so if you can't afford to join the dating website or don't feel that a kick boxing club is right for you, go back to spirit and ask again.

Writing things down and filling in a diagram only serve to focus our attention on the things that are the most important. Rather than just drifting and feeling as though we are being swept along, it gives us the chance to really think about what we are doing and where we want to be. It doesn't have to be a chore. It should be an opportunity for you to check in with your soul to see if you are on the right track. Things that you may have thought were important to you may become less so. The practice sessions in this book are just a mechanism to help you to look at your life in fresh ways. Your soul needs to find a way to talk to you, and by taking part in these exercises you have a chance to try another form of dialogue.

Feeling the Guilt
There is one thing we should clear up now. There appears to be a school of thought that says that you must be poor to be spiritual. Many of our religious leaders have been described as having little or nothing and are seen to give everything away. Consequently, it can seem incongruous to talk about money and spirituality in the same sentence. Having experienced worrying about how to pay the next bill and how I could possibly afford to buy anything healthy for my children to eat with what was left, I can honestly say that being poor sapped all my energy. I didn't have time to be spiritual when I was

running so fast to stand still. I always had a vision for myself and my family, which included living in a nice house and having enough money to pay the bills. Those things were important to me. I wanted to create a nice warm and pleasant environment for myself and my family to grow. Just before my 40th birthday, having spent years doing everything I thought was right, I started to get angry. I literally shouted out to spirit, "I know what poor feels like!! And I now want to know what it feels like not to have to keep worrying about money!". Clearly they were listening, because shortly after that my life started to change. Having studied for years, I was offered a job that put me on track to achieve my aims and although my anger was anything but spiritual, it did mark the start of a very important change.

If you want a nice house then you want a nice house. If you want a sports car then you want a sports car. The important thing is to think WHY you want those things. What will they bring to your life? The house was important to me because I wanted to live in an area where I could send my children to a school where they could fulfil their potential. I wanted space to dance (yes, really) and where I could be creative with interior design. I definitely didn't want the house in order to try to improve my social status: I wanted it to enhance my life in other ways. I knew those things would make me happy, but at the same time I didn't want to be struggling to pay all the bills. We live in a physical world and having some of the things that you really want does not make you any less spiritual. Equally, being poor does not make you any more spiritual either.

So whatever your hopes and wishes are for yourself, don't feel guilty about them. Understand why they are important and be prepared to change your mind. If your vision for yourself is in line with what your soul believes is in your best interests, then the path to achieving your goals will be made easier for you. Sometimes it is just a matter of timing. Sometimes it is because your belief system is preventing you from achieving what you really want.

GUIDANCE FROM THE OTHER SIDE

Being envious of what other people have in their lives has the effect of bringing your own energy down and, as we know, what you give out is what you get back. It is far nicer to share the joy when a friend has something you aspire to have in your life too. The likelihood is that they have had to work very hard for everything they have and sharing that joy with them is one of the nicest things you can do. They will be able to feel it (just as they can feel your envy) and they will be much more prepared to share the love.

HAVING A CLEAR VISION

Why you need one
You wouldn't get into a car or on to a train or a bus without having some destination in mind. At some point prior to travelling you will have decided that you would like to go somewhere and you will have your reasons. You might be driving because you feel as though you must, because it will benefit someone else; it could be for work or it could be for pleasure. You will be travelling for lots of different reasons, but in almost all cases there will be a purpose to your journey. It would be a rare thing if you suddenly got up out of your chair and walked to the bus stop without asking yourself why.

So why do we feel so comfortable travelling through life without having an aim in mind? Why do we deny our wishes and desires and settle for what other people think is good for us, or what we have become to believe is our only choice? We have free will and yet we often forget to use it.

In the non-physical realm, we use our free will to create what we want around us. Essentially, we think it and it is there. This happens almost instantaneously. We literally create it (or rather the illusion of it) as we decide what we want. When we first return to the realm after death, we might wish to recreate much of what we had on earth: where we lived, or somewhere we wanted to live; a familiar landscape, a garden full of beautiful flowers that we would enjoying looking after, a workshop full of familiar tools. There are no rules, we can create whatever we want. Eventually once back in the spirit world with earthly considerations fading behind us, we might decide we do not need some of the things we thought we needed and chose to create something else. It is entirely up to us.

Even though we are alive and living this spiritual existence in a physical body, we can still create. What is more we **should** create. Time is not measured in the spirit world, but here on earth it is. Living on earth we do not expect everything to happen in the blink of an eye, but often the time lag between deciding that you want something in your life and it appearing can be quite short. Unfortunately, we don't always recognise it for what it is. We sometimes block things thinking that we are not worthy, or that they were meant for someone else. Often we just haven't thought clearly enough about what we need in our lives and what those things actually look like; not in enough detail, anyway.

This general concept is not new in spiritual circles. There are several very well-respected publications which suggest this approach: *Creative Visualization* (Gawain S., 1978); *Ask and It Is Given* (Hicks E. & J., 2004); *The Secret* (Byrne, 2006), to name just three. Despite the name of the last one, this isn't actually a secret, nor should it be. This approach is open to everyone. As you have probably guessed, not everyone who has read these works has had their creative wants and desires met immediately. It might be easy for them to blame themselves: they didn't want it enough; they didn't focus enough; they are not worthy enough – that's rubbish by the way! Anything that puts any blame back towards the creator needs to be banished straight away. This is not a reward for good behaviour. This is about you deciding for yourself what your vision for the future should be. It is about liaising with yourself and deciding what you really want in your life. It is about understanding exactly why you want a particular thing. What will its materialisation mean for your life? How will it enhance what you already have? You also need to understand all the different forms that it might take when it does appear in your life.

This point reminds me of a popular joke: there is a town that suffers the most awful sudden flooding and people must be evacuated from their homes. One deeply religious man decides that his best chance of survival is to climb out of his bedroom window and up onto the roof of his house to wait for the water to subside. He is very afraid and turns his face up to the heavens to ask God for help. "Please God, save me!" He pleads for God to listen and repeats his heartfelt request, never doubting that he would be heard. Shortly afterwards a small rubber dinghy is seen in the distance and the occupant keenly wants to help him. Not fancying his chances in the dinghy, the man declines the offer saying that "God will save him". Shortly afterwards there are some rescuers in a rowing boat and they plead with him to get in. Again, not wishing to take a chance on the water, he declines the offer and the helpers decide to look for more willing people to rescue. Understanding his reluctance to escape via the water, the rescuers then ask for a helicopter to fly over his house to rescue the man but again, the man who is so certain that God will save him, declines the offer of being hauled up by a rope and on to dry land. Eventually the water washes up over the house and the man drowns. On reaching heaven the man is very angry: "God, why didn't you save me?" God replies: "I tried! I sent you a dinghy, a rowing boat and finally a helicopter!" In other words, if you ask for something, you must be open to the many forms in which your request may be granted. If the man was expecting to stay where he was until the water subsided, then he was lost. If, on the other hand, he had recognised that what he really wanted was to live, then he might have accepted one of the three methods on offer.

You might wonder how this tale might relate to the things that you want in your life: meeting the person of your dreams, for example. That may be about really analysing what you actually, truly want. If you are vague about what you are looking for, or haven't really thought it through, then you might not recognise when the right person comes along. To understand what you want, you have to completely understand yourself. To be loved you have to feel worthy of love; in short, you have to love yourself. This isn't about settling for just anything, it is about deciding what is really important to you personally. If you doggedly stick to someone else's idea of the perfect partner then you are in danger of not recognising your perfect partner when they come along. Fortunately your soul self knows what is right for you if you only listen. For example, what does the perfect partner look like to you? If you look for qualities, rather than wanting someone who has, say, a professional job, drives an expensive car, does not have children, travels the world and eats in expensive restaurants, etc. – you are more likely to find them. Why must they have a professional job, for example? Is it because you want them to be financially independent? Is it because you feel only someone with a professional job will be your intellectual equal? Maybe it is because you have a professional job and you want someone to contribute equally to living expenses? What do you think of as "professional", for example? Are you expecting a lawyer or a doctor? If you are not contemplating anyone who does not appear to you to have a professional job, then are you missing all the wonderful people who could make you happy? Having a professional job isn't always a measure of intellectual ability, either!

By focusing on qualities rather than achievements you leave the door open. Most people are looking for kindness, loyalty, interests in common as a basic starting-point. Yes, in this case looks are important too, but someone who takes care of their appearance might lead you to love, rather than the expectation of a particular look. Wanting someone who is good with money, rather than someone who drives an expensive car, might be closer to your aim of being financially independent, for example. But this is your vision and if, for example, you adore horses and they are the most important thing in your life, then it is clear that you will want someone who shares your passion. This is your vision of the perfect partner, but someone who respects and understands your vision but isn't currently involved in horses might be ideal, too. So don't be like the man on the roof – be open to all possibilities.

DECIDING WHAT YOUR VISION SHOULD BE

Loving who you are
As you have probably gathered by now, deciding what your vision for yourself should be is not that easy. Firstly, go back into your light-filled bubble and pose the question to your soul self.

If you are looking for love, what qualities that you find in yourself do you love? Is it your compassion, your kindness, your understanding of animals? Is it your sense of fun? Maybe you love the fact that you are hard-working, but still find the time to help others? It is essential to understand who you are before you can think about what you want. If something is key to your personality then it is important to recognise it and consider how another person would honour this aspect of yourself.

If you are family-oriented, what does that actually mean to you? Does it mean that you love your parents and extended family but are happy to see them once a year, or does it mean that you will always want to live close to your family and stay in your home town? Maybe you love your family dearly, but you are looking for your own adventure. Perhaps you want to travel the world and keep in touch with home via technology for a few months at a time. Both versions of yourself could be called "family-oriented" but they are polar opposites in terms of how you want to spend your life. Perhaps you fall somewhere between the two? Perhaps you already have responsibility for children and they will shape your future life. You don't necessarily have to find someone who is in the same position, just someone who is sensitive to your situation and who is prepared to work with it. You need someone who will understand if you have to give up a much-anticipated romantic break because your child suddenly becomes ill and can't be left with a relative. As much as you might want to put your new partner first, you have a deep sense of responsibility and someone who respects and understands that is on the "must-have" list. There is no right or wrong list – there is just YOUR list. The more you understand about yourself, the more likely you are to recognise your new love when they turn up! This is assuming that you even want another significant person in your life, of course. Loving who you are for yourself, not as a reflection of yourself in others, is a very important outcome.

You must be completely honest with yourself. In doing so, what is it that you do not like about yourself? Are you likely to reject someone if you feel they are judging you? Notice I am saying "feel they are judging you": they may not be, but your insecurities may be preventing you from seeing the true situation. You must come to terms with what you like less about yourself, too. Be clear about this: it is not another opportunity to metaphorically beat yourself up about some of your less desirable features. You are living in a physical world and you are not perfect, but then neither is anyone else. As spiritual beings we should be aiming to be the best version of ourselves possible – think of those spiritual qualities of kindness, compassion, understanding, empathy, gratitude, enthusiasm, positivity – and love. Being the most empathetic and compassionate version of ourselves is a worthy activity. Criticising yourself because you do not live up to unrealistic stereotypes is not.

The phrase "love yourself" is banded about quite freely these days, but when you feel worn out, need to wash your hair and are feeling guilty about what the kids have eaten or not eaten this week, it's easier said than done. Loving yourself could be so far down your list of things to do that it rarely gets a look-in. Don't be too hard on yourself. I honestly believe that everyone is inherently good. The goodness in some people can be more difficult to find, but it is there. You possess many excellent qualities. You are energy living a physical existence in a less than perfect world. To love yourself you will need to rise above all the things which you think you should be and reassess each and every one.

Sitting in your bubble, go back to thinking about those spiritual qualities of kindness, compassion, understanding, empathy, gratitude, enthusiasm, positivity and love and ask yourself how you measure up to those. Most of those qualities are linked; kindness often comes from empathy and compassion for others, and for that you need understanding. If you are grateful for what you already have then that helps you to be enthusiastic and positive about the future. Love underpins all of those qualities and is the path to loving yourself. Sounds impossible? It isn't. You just have to take one day at a time. You just need to find some space in your head to accept that you are doing your best in this imperfect world and then check yourself as often as you can to make sure that you are holding on to those qualities as best you can.

When you start to love yourself you can start to be loved. You can't have one without the other. If the words "love yourself" feel too strong and self-indulgent for you then replace them with "respect and care for yourself". If you can't do that for yourself, how can you expect anyone else to do it for you?

Once again, just because a lot of people feel as though their future vision has to include a romantic partnership, that does not imply that you need to be looking for one as well. Being a totally self-sufficient, strong and independent person AND not feeling as though sharing your life with another person is going to enhance it is a preferred state for many people.

Decide the Life You Want

If you have taken the time to go through the process above, you should have a much better idea about what is important to you. At this point, you should be developing a much better idea about what you want. Now would be a good time to record those thoughts.

Get a piece of paper or sit at a laptop, whatever you are most comfortable with, and make some serious notes. You need space for this, so I am not suggesting that you just tap notes into your phone at this stage. It may help to think about your vision under the following headings: relationships; career/job; family; finances; social activity. It's your list, so you can rename, add or remove sections as you wish. These are just basic suggestions which might cover what many people want to think about.

This is a process that should not be rushed. It is your opportunity to sit down and really think about the dream you have for yourself. So I am suggesting that you record your thoughts and ideas in some detail. There is more information in Resources (Section E). When recording your vision, make sure that the wording makes it sound as though these things are already in your life now. By writing in the present tense, you are aligning your current and future energies.

Relationships

Relationships can take many forms. It can be the relationship you have with all the members of your family, your work colleagues and friends. If there are several different areas you want to look at that come under the heading of "relationships", pick just one or two for now. You will know by now which are the most important to you. Maybe you feel as though you are not gelling well with someone at work and this is making your working life more difficult. It could be a strained relationship with a sibling or parent, it could be a complex relationship with one particular friend. You can decide where to focus this attention.

GUIDANCE FROM THE OTHER SIDE

Write down your ideal relationship with the person you would like to get on better with. What positive qualities does this person possess? What do you love about them? How does knowing this person make you feel? Write this in the present tense as though that is what life is like now. By writing as if you already have the relationship you desire, you are creating an energy around you that will bring the desired situation closer to you. On an energy level, like attracts like. So if you are describing a relationship that is fulfilling for you, then you are putting your energy at the right level to attract it. If, however, you focus on what is missing in your current relationship, especially if you cover old ground about what is wrong with so and so, then you are creating an energy of "lack". That is to say, you are focusing on what is missing in your life rather than what is good in it. We are energetic beings and we are full of great qualities which we want to attract to ourselves: in this case, in the form of other people we come into contact with. If we put out the right energy then we attract that right energy back towards us. If you are struggling, try connecting again with your soul self to understand what sort of relationship is the most beneficial for you with the people you are thinking about.

Career/Job

Be careful here how you formulate and word your ideal career or job. I used to set an exercise very similar to this to first-year undergraduate students as part of a professional development module. The aim was to get them to think very carefully about what their future career aims were so that they would have a clear vision for themselves that would keep them motivated over the next three years. Initial discussions might centre on what a good career would buy for them: a big house, a fast car, etc., but when we started to dig deeper it was more about what these material items represented. The big house was to provide stability for a future growing family, or it might be to make their parents proud. The fast car was often more about gaining respect from their peers than actually wanting to drive at any great speed. It was not true in all cases, of course: an engineering student might appreciate the specific features of one particular model of car over another and have very clear technical reasons why they wanted it.

It became clear when talking to some students that they were following career plans set out by their parents, rather than having made any decisions themselves about what they ultimately wanted to do. If you are following someone else's dream rather than your own, it is often difficult to keep the momentum going when things get tough. Eventually you will start to question why you are following a particular path and whether it truly represents who you are. Some students would even write that they wanted to work hard – up to 100 hours a week! That is quite a vision to set for yourself. I think what they really wanted was energy and focus, but in asking the universe to give you a job where you will be working 100 hours per week, you need to analyse if that is what you really desire, because those hours will impact on every other area of your life.

This is an opportunity to dream big. Do not feel limited by your starting-point or the enormity of the goal in front of you. There are many examples of celebrities, sports personalities and entrepreneurs who will tell you that they started from very humble beginnings. What they all have in common is that they had a dream. Many people along the way will have told them to "get real" and not to be too ambitious or get "above themselves", but their dream and certainty that they could make it happen saw them through.

There are some things to consider here, though. Not everyone who wants to become a professional footballer will be chosen to play for an elite club. Not every good singer will receive a recording contract and make millions – but some will. Do any of those who reach the top of their profession ever do that without first having a dream that seemed impossible at the time? If you want to be a professional footballer, be honest with yourself and ask why that accolade is so important to you. Is it for the adulation? If so, what form should that take? More importantly, why is that sort of adulation so important to you? If you analyse your motives and you are honest about it, there may be other opportunities open to you along the way which you will find just as fulfilling. Do not be put off by one or two people telling you something will never happen if you believe that it will. But be very clear about what a specific career will do for you, and be open to other options.

It is far better to look at the qualities you need to fulfil your career aim and think how those qualities feel to you. Imagine a day, even a week, as a professional footballer. What would life be like? Are you the sort of person who would thrive on the uncertainty, or would you prefer something more stable? Would you enjoy the limelight or would you prefer to go for a meal with friends without someone recognising you? There are many opportunities and jobs around that you may not even be aware of today. If you are still young then in twenty or even in ten years' time there will be new jobs and opportunities which we cannot even imagine. If you understand yourself and your desires you can complete this section in broader terms such as "I am working with elite sports people"; "I am at my peak of physical fitness"; "I am earning enough money to provide a comfortable lifestyle that will enable me to (fill in the gaps)".

Family
Family may take many forms and the people we consider family are often not formally related by birth or marriage. Over time, dear friends become family and depending on our jobs, we can sometimes have a work family as well. Whatever your personal definition of family, you can decide for yourself. We are all family in an energy sense. We are all from one source and we really are all one, so it makes no difference at all.

Many people interpret this as starting or having their own family, so this is the place to think whether having children is in your ideal plan. Not everyone is lucky enough to welcome their own baby into their lives and you may know already that even though this would be your ideal, for you personally it is not an option. It is therefore important to take a broad view of this section as well. What things would you ideally like to experience as parent, or in a parent-style role? Is it being able to guide an older child, or is it the opportunity to join in creative play? If you think exactly what you would like to experience and leave the possibility open to being able to enjoy some of these things, even if you are not fortunate enough to have a child of your own, you are leaving the door open. If you really do hope to have a child or children then add that to your list. Long before I became a parent myself, I wrote on my vision list that I would like two children, a boy and a girl. I was lucky enough to achieve that goal.

When giving this exercise to students, one particularly compassionate girl said that she wanted to always look after her mum. Although the sentiment was lovely, I couldn't help thinking that it might have been better to wish very good health for her mum, and that she could see and support her mum whenever she wanted. By setting a wish to "always look after someone" you are setting an intention to be a carer, whether that was your original intention or not.

When thinking about family, thoughts often turn to where you might want to live. What sort of property would you like? Again, rather than saying you want a house on a particular street, think about how the house would make you feel. You may want to feel that there is enough room to dance, as I did, or that you want to feel safe and secure. You may want a light-filled house, or one that feels cosy and warm. By focusing on how your ideal property will make you feel you are more likely to recognise the feeling when you find it. If you are fixed on an idea that you want a detached house, or a mansion that overlooks mountains on one side and the sea on the other, you are missing places which are not like that, but which could make you very happy. That is not to say that you might not get your mansion and it might be exactly as you have imagined it. Believe me, this is more than possible when working with energies, but it could be that your soul self knows that you could be very happy in other places as well. So really think about it and if you want your house to be set away from other houses, ask yourself why. Typical answers might be that you want to be quiet and another family living in close proximity would not be right for you. Make sure that your reasons are clear: if you want the mansion just to show some of your family and friends that you are successful then those thoughts do not necessarily serve you. If you want a mansion because it means you can open it up to all sorts of activities which will benefit others, and if it complements your life plan, that is a definite reason for wanting a such a property.

There is absolutely nothing wrong with wanting the best for yourself. You should: you are most definitely worth it, and your soul self wants the best for you as well. Just be very clear about your intentions. Analyse your motivations and be open to your wishes being granted in a variety of ways.

Finances
I think it is fair to say that most people don't want to have to worry about money. It saps your energy, as I have said before, and while you are thinking about how to pay the next bill or worried that something you have will be taken away from you, you can't think about anything else in your life. The question here is how much money you want or need, and for everyone the answer will be different. A standard answer is that people want to be "comfortable", but that means different things to different people, too.

The starting-point is normally having enough money to pay all your bills, but on top of that you need to think about the sort of lifestyle you want. It may be your aim not to work at all! Or at the very least for as few hours a week as possible. Working very hard and working very long hours does not necessarily make you rich, not even in monetary terms. The reality is often quite the opposite. It is not always helpful to put an exact figure on the amount you want to earn: it will be much easier to think about the lifestyle you ideally want and consider all the things you want to do; the more detail, the better. Money represents security for a lot of people and for others it might represent freedom and adventure. There are many ways to achieve your dreams, and that could include working for part of the year and travelling for the rest. In such a case, a large and expensive house to support may not be on the agenda – it is your dream and if you sit within your light filed bubble and really try and connect, you true soul self will give you some very big clues about what will make you happy.

We are energy and everything around us is made up of energy and money has an energy all of its own. Paper money that we are now using less and less is handed round from person to person – each piece holding an intention of how it should be spent. Now we rarely get to handle the money we spend and what we are doing is spending a form of trust. We spend according to the intention that we have for the funds we have available – or not available, as the case may be. We need to make sure that those intentions are pure and that the money (or energy) we spend to bring things to us is right for us. We don't need everything we can perceive. We just need what is right for us at this moment.

Social Activity

This section covers everything else. What makes you, you? How do you like/want to spend your time? What makes you happy? This section may include much more modest aims, such as meeting with friends at the weekend and enjoying a simple lunch. Not everything you wish for needs to be exotic or what others might think of as "exciting".

Your soul self just wants you to be happy. That's all, that's it. Think back to the times you have been at your happiest. What were you doing? Who were you with? You may be surprised to find that you were doing something quite simple and probably even free.

GUIDANCE FROM THE OTHER SIDE

Not everyone wants to swim with dolphins – I certainly don't! If travel is important to you, think very carefully about the type of places you do want to visit. What things will you do when you get there? What kind of traveller are you: adventurous and prepared to manage with very little on your journey, or do you want a home from home and all modern comforts? People have very different ideas about travelling and now is the time to think about yours.

Social activity includes hobbies and sport, too, unless those things are so important to you that you have made them into a section on their own. Only you know what should be included in here. Be as specific as you can and decide from your heart by being guided by your soul self. We are all different, we do not all want the same things, but you can dream big – in fact you should!

Be Careful What You Wish For
As an energetic being you can attract many things into your life that you want – you are much more powerful than you realise, which is why it is important to think very carefully about what you wish for. Be careful about how you word things and always write in the present tense as though you already have those things. If you write "I want" then you could be given exactly what you "want", which is to be left wanting. So if you say "I want more free time" then the universe will leave you wanting more free time, because that is what you have asked for. If you say "I enjoy lots of free time to see my musical friends and play my guitar with them" then you are connecting with the energy of meeting friends and making music together, and because the energy and the physical manifestation of it are almost the same thing you are much more likely to achieve it. As you write and repeat the words "I enjoy lots of free time to see my musical friends and play my guitar with them", your soul self works on how that will happen. You may suddenly become aware of a poster in your music shop that had

hitherto gone unnoticed about an event you might find interesting, and at the event you might overhear a conversation about a group of people who are looking for someone to play guitar with them. How your dreams manifest themselves can take different forms and all you really need to do is to hold the energy and be open to the infinite possibilities. Consequently, be absolutely certain that you have given a great deal of thought about what you really want, because you will be surprised how quickly these things can happen if you are open to them.

Sometimes the dreams that we initially have for ourselves may not be in exact alignment with what the universe and our soul self have in mind, but they can be very important stepping-stones along the way. In any case, some of the things we initially wish for ourselves may not be what we eventually decide we need when we understand more about ourselves and the process.

The universe sometimes has a habit of putting us on a training course of which we might not initially see the purpose, but it turns out to be essential in the end. To use my own experience as an example, during my teens I studied acting and drama. I went to a stage school and had some experience of acting at the local but sizeable theatre, and playing a role in a few shows. For a few months the thought of being a professional actor fleetingly crossed my mind, but I knew deep down that my heart wasn't really in it enough to make it a full-time career. A waste of time, then? Not at all! When I started teaching, all those voice projection classes and acting lessons gave me the confidence to stand up in a room of often hundreds of people and start talking. Not a natural extrovert, I thought of teaching as acting until I became sufficiently comfortable with the sea of faces looking back at me for hours on end. Once I remember reading about a successful and very accomplished cosmetic surgeon who had been an absolute wizard in her school sewing class. All those hours spent learning how to make the neatest stitches had provided an excellent training ground for her eventual career. So the path to your final dream may not necessarily take a direct route. This does not mean that you have failed in any way, it just means that your soul self might have something slightly different in mind for you. Be sure, though, that the aim is always the same – to allow your soul to grow and provide the experiences it needs for progression.

Sabotaging the Vision, and How Not To
By the time you have recorded your vision, you should have a detailed list of your hopes, wishes and dreams for yourself. All good, then? Well, it should be, but as spiritual beings living a physical existence we have a habit of sabotaging our best efforts. It is almost as though our logical earth-bound brain wants to challenge our soul self and feed it with doubt. We challenge ourselves by asking how and why we dare to dream. Our logical brain doesn't want to risk being disappointed, so it starts to point out all the "good" things about staying exactly where we are. It wants us to believe that it will be easier and safer to do nothing. It starts to question our ability to achieve what we have set out to do and points out that we are not talented or clever enough to achieve these aims. If we have a dream of starting a business then it starts to question how successful we shall be, and whether we have the skills to do it. The list will go on and on as long as we let it. The important thing here is to recognise it for what it is, but then learn from it.

If, for example, your dream is to be a singer and win one of the famous talents shows that are regularly televised, have you analysed what qualities the winners of those shows typically have? Are they singer-songwriters? Do they have another skill along with singing? You do not have to be the same as them, but it helps to have an understanding about what makes them successful if your aim is as specific as that. If the very successful ones write their own songs, have you tried doing that? What sort of songs are meaningful to you personally? Can you offer something different? If your aim is to have your own business and you have a particular idea in mind, learn everything you possibly can about the sector you are interested in. Find out about sources of finance and really do your homework. Your soul self wants to help you, but you do have to put the effort in.

The more you align your energy with what you want to achieve by finding out more about your dream and building up a clearer picture, the closer you become to it. If your logical brain is throwing up doubts, do not give up. Use those doubts to learn and, if necessary, progress your dreams into something more substantial. Listen to advice – really listen. When you work more closely with the spirit world, you will be sent what you need when you need it. It might be hearing a chance conversation, or finding just the right book. It could be finding "by chance" a YouTube video that answers some of your questions. Be prepared for your dreams to be refined and clarified into something even more powerful than you originally intended.

Just before we leave this section, there is another way of sabotaging your dreams that you need to be aware of. Sometimes we hold preconceived ideas about what achieving our dreams will be like and we may wish to avoid some of those things. Going back to the example of someone setting up their own business and becoming very successful, we may sabotage this dream for ourselves because we hold some negative ideas about what a very successful person is like. We may believe on a subconscious level that to be very successful you have to be ruthless, heartless and be prepared to tread on people on your way to the top. You may believe that in order to be successful you will have no time for your family and that people will be jealous of you and not wish you well. If you hold false thoughts such as these, and you do not identify those qualities in yourself, you will almost certainly not achieve your aim to be a successful businessperson.

To combat these thoughts, return to your light-filled bubble and really examine any prejudices you might have. Think about where they have come from. Perhaps you have met, or been told about, a successful person who has acted in a negative way. Sometimes these thoughts go way back, even possibly to a past life, but they do not necessarily represent things as they are now. Decide how representative and true these views really are. You will need to examine each and every one of them and decide what to do about it. You do not have to follow that negative pattern of success – this is your dream. You can be a very successful person who is kind and altruistic. You can create a business that provides good opportunities and excellent conditions for employees, and one that does a great deal for the community.

Sabotaging can apply to relationships, too. If you don't love and respect yourself, you might lack the love and respect for someone who loves you. Perhaps you have a few negative ideas about being in a couple: where have those ideas come from? Does this go back to your parents, or are you focusing on other relationships which have ended up with people going their separate ways? If you have few examples of successful relationships in your immediate circle, it might be difficult to believe that any couple can stay together and be happy for 30, 40, 50 or even 60 years. We tend to hear about the negative outcomes and statistics are used as attention-grabbing headlines to warn us how many marriages end in divorce. We hear far less about the successful relationships and the happy couples who are delighted and feel very fortunate to have spent most of their lives together. If you are looking for love (though there is no reason why you need to be unless you particularly want to), analyse those preconceived ideas – especially if deep down you are worried that a long-term relationship will be stifling and stop you from doing what you really want. It does not have to be like that – you are writing your own dream. Write the sort of loving relationship that you want. Read about what makes a successful relationship and about couples who have made it. You also need to make time in your life to share with someone else. Sometimes our logical brains fill up our time so much that there is no time for anyone else. Knowledge is power. Really think about where these negative influences are coming from and find some balance. For further ideas, have a look at Resources (Section F).

Chapter 2 Summary: Establishing a Clear Vision

- Decide what is important:
    - Distinguish between what you want and need in material terms and how you want to feel
    - The universe supports a path in line with what our soul wants
    - Get help if you need it, but decide to be happy now if you can
    - Focus on joy and gratitude, rather than what is missing in your life
    - Use the tools to identify where you need to focus your attention
    - Being poor does not make you more spiritual

- In the spirit world we use our free will to create what we want around us.

- If we have a clear vision while living in the physical realm, we can still use our free will to create a lot of what we want in our lives:
    - Be crystal clear about what you want and why you want it; this involves understanding yourself
    - Be open to the many forms that creating your vision might take
- Decide the life you want:
    - Describe your ideal life in as much detail as possible as though it has already happened by writing in the present tense
    - Like attracts like and the energy you give out is what will be reflected back to you
    - Your soul self wants you to be happy so dream big, but make sure it is what you truly want
    - Don't sabotage your dreams by hanging onto subliminal negative ideas about what achieving your dreams might involve.

CHAPTER 3
HARNESSING INNER GUIDANCE

THE CONCEPT OF ENOUGH

By connecting with our soul selves, it will become much easier to decide how much we need in our lives: what is surplus to requirements and what can be given a new life – either with us or with others. There are only so many clothes we can wear, pots we can cook with or objects we can place on shelves. We need to ensure that we only surround ourselves with things which lift our energies and ultimately make us happy. At that point, we need to stop.

We are constantly bombarded by advertisements which promise happiness through the purchase of some item or other. We know that we are being manipulated, but we enjoy the process so, generally, we are happy to engage with it. Advertising is so much more subtle these days, with lifestyle gurus and other influencers encouraging us to buy into a lifestyle that other people tell us is what we should aspire to. We know deep down that this is crazy, but for some reason we follow the crowd and tell ourselves that we need things which, in themselves, have absolutely no capacity to change our lives.

All we need to do is to break the cycle. All we need to do is to switch the focus from following to leading. What do we really need in our lives? What will enhance our space? What will make us happy? We are not the same, so what I decide is essential will and should be different to the things you wish to have in your life. There is no universal ideal – just what is ideal for us. For example, I have always had an interest in interior design and consequently, the changes that I make to my home in terms of interiors make me very happy indeed. I derive enormous pleasure from planning a scheme, painting or wallpapering walls and making the space feel special. This is such a fundamental part of who I am that to deny myself this would not make me happy. We should allow ourselves to be joyful and happy; there is absolutely nothing wrong with that.

The key element here is "enough". I have reached a point where I can enjoy looking at beautiful interiors without feeling the need to change things just because I have seen the latest design. My focus is this: will this latest item enhance my space and make me happier than I am now? This puts me in charge, rather than the random marketeers who have sales quotas to fill. Everyone who sells seems to have a backstory these days. In fact, a backstory and a lifestyle that can be promoted online is an essential sales technique. We must recognise these things for what they are and then say "enough". My "enough" might be different to your "enough" and that really doesn't matter, provided we both stop at that point and ask ourselves if surrounding ourselves with yet more stuff will make us happy.

Clearing Space
Connecting to your soul self requires you to make space in your head so that you can make these decisions. To be able to truly listen to your inner voice, you need to clear everyday noise. That includes not just actual environmental outside noise and noise that is created by anyone you live with; you also need to clear the noise created by random thoughts and worries which compete for attention in your head. As discussed earlier, anyone who has tried to meditate will know that banishing random thoughts is not necessarily all that easy.

During our lives we do not always have the luxury of being able to control the physical space around us and if we are in this position, we must respect the belongings of others and attempt to compromise. If, on the other hand, we can make decisions about where we live and what physical items surround us, then we can consider clearing the space.

GUIDANCE FROM THE OTHER SIDE

A great deal has been written about decluttering and I shall talk more about this shortly, but clearing space or "space clearing" has many more implications than just throwing out a few old jumpers. Everything that we bring into our personal environment has energy. If we want to feel that spiritual connection then it helps if we clear out anything that has negative connotations for us, and to do that we need to be able to recognise what those items are.

If you take a moment to look around you, notice what items are in your immediate vicinity. Perhaps you already adopt a very minimalist lifestyle and only surround yourself with items which are meaningful for you and bring you joy. If that is the case then this section of the book may not be for you but before you skip this section, ask yourself how the items that are in the room with you, *feel* to you. It might seem an odd thing to ask and can take a bit of time to answer to but do those things lift your spirits? Do they make you happy?

Perhaps you are sharing your space with some very necessary practical and essential items such as a laptop, household filing or paperwork for your job. Maybe you have items that you would not have chosen, but which have been bought for you as presents: you may not love the object but you love the person who bought it. There are so many reasons why we end up being surrounded by the things that we do. Sometimes we inherit objects from long passed family and they represent an enduring connection to them. The thought of parting with those objects might feel like parting from your loved one all over again.

Often the things we inherit were never intended to be passed down the generations and I sometimes think that spirit people might be quite amused at what we revere that they left behind. When they originally bought the item many years previously, what would they have thought if they had known it would still be around 50 or 100 years later? The thing that you buy today, do you expect anyone in your family to have it sitting on their bookshelf in 80 years' time? When we have to consider sustainability, maybe we should be thinking in this way, but you could be holding on to a particularly ugly vase bought for your granny by a neighbour, which your granny never really liked! If you have bought everything yourself and have had the chance to choose things that you love, then there is every chance that you are already only surrounded by objects which lift your spirits and enhance your space. If you can look round your room and be sure that is the case, then please skip this section – it is not for you.

While sitting in your chair, look in turn at as many items as you can. Try to detach ideas of practicality and sentiment and ask yourself what you feel when you look at them. You may need to do this a few times, but even if you are surrounded by very few items, make sure they lift your spirits rather than bringing them down. Some items will just feel "neutral" and that is fine for now. Not everything in your home will evoke an emotional response. If it does feel neutral to you, ask yourself if it has a practical purpose.

The Process of Clearing Space
If you are looking around your room and acknowledging that your space is being invaded by too many things which attempt to deplete your energy, then take heart because there is a great deal you can do to improve the situation. No one is expecting you to get rid of all your belongings and sit cross-legged on the floor in an empty room. We cannot take anything with us when we leave this physical life but certainly our physical lives can be made more comfortable when we surround ourselves with things which we love and truly need.

Over the past few years, numerous authors have provided templates to show us how to declutter things from our life; if you know this is an issue for you then see which of these authors resonate with you. One of my particular favourites is Marie Kondo, with her YouTube videos and books encouraging us to *Spark Joy* (Kondo M., 2016) from the items which surround us. Marie Kondo pays tribute to the energy surrounding these objects by suggesting that we acknowledge that they have served us well and wish them well as we part with them. I particularly like this approach, as anything we do not want should be passed on with as many good energy vibrations as possible. I can wholeheartedly recommend the Spark Joy approach, and if you are serious about decluttering then her method is a good place to start.

For my part, I want to bring your attention to why you might be holding on to certain things and what they represent in your life. By connecting with our soul self, our thinking will start to change. For true transformation to take place, we must view things differently. Many of us buy material objects for other people to show that we care; this can be especially true of buying things for children. We can show that we care in so many other ways and concentrating on shared experiences rather than buying objects would be a new way to look at things.

We are energy, the items which we share our lives with are energy and the things which we want in our lives have energy. Like attracts like, so it is important that the energy that surrounds us is of the same energetic vibration as the things we wish to attract. That is not to say that we need to examine every mug, plate or kitchen utensil we possess to determine if it is of the same type of energy as the new partner we want to attract – obviously not; but we do need to be sensitive to things around us which might be bringing our energy down.

If when you walk into your home, for example, you are met with so much clutter in your hallway that you heart sinks – then that is clearly bringing down your energy as you enter a place that should uplift you and be your sanctuary. If you walk into a room and cannot push the door back to at least a right angle because your sofa is too big then that will be an annoyance every time you enter the room. If you are met with a picture that you inherited, but which is a depressing image then how can that make you anything other than depressed? The picture may have sentimental connotations because you inherited it from someone you love, but if it does not serve the space well then you should remove it.

Think of your home as your precious sanctuary. You deserve to feel safe and inspired in the place where you spend most of your time. If you share your home with others and cannot change most of it, then concentrate on the area around your bed or chair. Make sure it is clean and free of clutter to provide you with the head space you need to make positive and important life-enhancing changes in your life.

Why We Hold On To Stuff
We have a habit of going through life with a mental "to-do list" – some of these things must be done, such as paying bills, working for a living, etc., but then we have a tendency to fill our lives with "shoulds" which do not have the potential to enhance our lives. We "should" read that book we received for Christmas; we "should" go through that box of photographs and place them in an album in chronological order; we "should" finish that blanket we started crocheting ten years ago/rearrange tools in the garage or even clearing our electronic clutter. "Shoulds" bring our energy down, so we either need to decide to do those things now or we need to recategorize them as things we shall really enjoy doing over the next few weeks. If they do not make that list, we seriously need to think about whether they need doing at all.

The reasons we hold on to things are very complex. Often, they can represent who we either used to be or dearly aspire to be. By removing them, we are having to come to terms with the fact that we are no longer the person we identified with.

By way of example, imagine that you are very creative and you see yourself as fine artist. You have created some beautiful artwork in the past which you are happy with and for which you were given much praise, but for a variety of reasons you have not produced anything for a very long while. Producing more art is on your "should" list. You still have your old paints (some of them were drying up so you have bought more and they are lying unopened in a box under the bed). You have been tempted to try other creative pursuits and like the idea of working with textiles, so you have three boxes of interesting fabric in your attic so you can do something with that later. If many years have passed and your lack of creativity bothers you, then those items must bring your energy down every time you see them. Even if they are stored out of sight you know they are there, calling to you to do "something". It doesn't have to be art, it can be learning to play music, restoring a car or starting a business. Things we intended to do, which it was hoped would bring us pleasure, can end up being a burden and bringing our energy down every time we think about them. If we spend money on something then we feel guilty if we don't do something with it, because by getting rid of those things now we not only have to come to terms with not being who we thought we were but also the fact that we have "wasted our money" – and that throws up a whole load of guilt for so many people. So rather than face all this, we continue to hold on to the things which support the notion of who we aspire to be.

Do any of those examples resonate with you? If anyone says to you, "You haven't touched those paints in 15 years, get rid of them!" how will you react? How can they possibly understand that those paints represent far more than what they can see? By throwing them away you are telling yourself that you are no longer an artist. You are having to admit that a very important part of you is dead; you are not who you thought you were! So rather than that we put them back in the box under the bed, or in the attic, so that we can tell ourselves that we will do this one day.

My personal and metaphorical "box in the attic" is an exercise bike that I can honestly say I spent more time dusting than using! I moved it into more prominent positions around the house to encourage me to use it and yet nothing changed. I was asked to "Get rid of it, because you never use it and it's in the way" more times than I can remember. I resisted, initially because to me, getting rid of that bike felt like totally giving up and while it was still there it represented the real possibility of getting much fitter (and losing some weight!). In the end I accepted that with my dodgy and often painful knee, cycling was not the best exercise for me anyway. It was a lack of focus and general commitment to exercise that was preventing me from getting fitter, and that had absolutely nothing to do with the bike. The fact is, I can be fit or unfit depending on how much effort I am prepared to put in. The bike can't make me fitter – only I can do that.

If we aspire to be more than we are then what has stopped us? For some, there may be genuine and very justifiable reasons why fulfilling their dream is not possible at the moment. For others it might be that if they do allow themselves to try a particular skill, they might find out that they are not very good at it. Perhaps that early artwork was a fluke! Perhaps they will never produce anything so good again! If we try, we may have to confront our own fallibility and accept that if it does not work out as we expect, then we shall have to confront our fear that we are not who we thought we were. This can be very painful for a lot of people, so we hide away what we do not wish to confront. Of course, if we do try then we might be a great deal better than we thought, too – it can work both ways. In fact, why deny yourself the chance to prove that?

Not everyone will recognise this scenario, of course, but if you do then by connecting with your soul self and being prepared to learn, you can break the cycle. Analyse what has really stopped you from being who you want to be and decide to do something about it. If you feel creative, give yourself permission to be an artist. If you want to play guitar and join a band, make a start and think of yourself as a musician. Put these goals on your vision list and focus on being that person now. If, on the other hand, you realise that these goals no longer represent who you truly are, pass your paints onto someone else and focus on the things which will bring you joy now.

Sometimes the time isn't just quite right, or we are plainly "doing our best" and certainly should not feel pressured by other people into getting rid of something that we will regret later. Just being prepared to understand why you are holding on to things and what they represent for you may be enough for now.

Categories of Clutter
We hold on to some things for practical reasons, such as a scruffy pair of boots that are great in the snow; resources relating to our job; kitchenware that we maybe don't use very often, but it's great when we do. It is not good for the environment or our bank balance if we declutter things which we shall need later – the key element here is honesty. Too many items kept "just in case" constitute clutter that you must share your life with. How many of us have that drawer containing chargers and cables for phones or laptops which we no longer own? Do we even know what some of those things do? How difficult would it really be to get all your items of technology together and work out what cable goes with which product? Just by doing that one task you will start to feel more in control and your heart (and energy) will not drop every time you look in the drawer or can't find a charger.

Many of our belongings can be separated into groups and it helps to discuss those so that we can decide the response.

Work Items
If you are surrounded by paperwork representing work and stress it will be much more difficult to raise your energy, but there are steps you can take to rectify this. With many more people working from home these days, the line between work and home life can become much less clear. If you have

the opportunity to dedicate a specific room in your house to work-related activities, then you have the chance to shut the door on it when you have finished. If you don't have to use that room for anything else then you have a clear demarcation line when you leave. You are telling your higher self that work is done for the day and you are free to think about other things. Not everyone has this luxury, of course; even for those who do, finding that clear line between work and home life is never easy. The good news is that things can be done to draw that line and clear the space for something else.

The first thing to say is that work paraphernalia should be allocated its own space, even if it is in the smallest section of a room. If you are short of space, then just having a smart box in which to place your work items at the end of the day will suffice. You might move away from the space to work at different times, but there should be somewhere in your mind that is dedicated to work if you have to work from home, at least for part of the time. This is all about separating energies so that they don't overlap into other things which distract you and bring you down. It doesn't matter whether you love your work or find it a necessary chore, the principle is the same. You are providing your brain with a mechanism to set the intention that work be done.

If, for example, you have a dedicated study or office space in your home then it will help when closing the door behind you to say to yourself, "That's it until 8.30 am tomorrow", and then mentally lock the door – if you have a physical key to turn all the better, but it is the intention that is important.

Keeping paperwork out of sight will help you to relax, so if you can put your work away in an attractive box at the end of a working session this will have the same effect as closing a door. Set the intention that work time is over until the next session and hide it away as much as possible.

Books and Magazines

This category may or may not be related to work, but homes can be full of surplus paper screaming for attention. With so much online, it would be easy to argue that the best policy here is to read a book or magazine and then immediately pass it on to someone else. If you buy an electronic copy, cloud storage isn't taking up any physical space so this could be a very good solution for a physical decluttering of books you might want to read later. Although it could be argued that electronic clutter is still "a thing", and anyone – such as myself – who hasn't cleared out their email inbox for a while could be accused of having electronic clutter. Charity shops still accept books and book depositories are a great idea if you want to leave a book and take another one for free. I will be honest here and say that personally, I can only aspire to this model. As an ex-academic I have a particular fondness for physical books and a one-year rule for magazines. The reasoning is that magazines are designed to be topical, so the knowledge contained inside is already out of date after a year. I have a friend who joyfully passes magazines onto me the same month that they come out – I admire her so much for that, but I can only aspire to this level of discipline. I use magazines as an inspirational resource and derive so much pleasure from flicking over the pages, but I would like to get my one-year rule down to six (ideally three) months maximum so that I can pass them on to other people whilst they are still topical.

Nevertheless, over the years I have passed on literally hundreds of books to charities and I can honestly say that I have not missed any of them. The ones I have kept are the ones I have particular fondness for; they are almost exclusively on metaphysical subjects and some of them are no longer in print. I don't keep books and magazines for the sake of filing up a bookshelf. I think about which ones I really want for either reference or for the joy of reading again. To give a feeling of space, all my books are in one spot and enclosed behind doors. If I am looking for a particular title, I can normally find it, so to me, this isn't clutter.

You need to decide what constitutes clutter for you. If something gives you joy when you look at it, and you know that you will want to see it or use it again, then hold on to it. If you do not feel the joy response when you look at it then ask yourself if someone else can make better use of it. If you have hundreds of books and you love each and every one of them, then that isn't clutter to you. If you have a thousand books which you have accumulated and many of them are no longer relevant in your life, and you know that you will never want to read them again, pass them on to a charity or otherwise dispose of them sympathetically to someone who wants them, and make room in your life for some new knowledge to come in. The general thinking here is that by leaving spaces on your bookshelves you are inviting new knowledge to come to you.

Clothing
Fast fashion is of significant concern to a great many people and moving forward through the 21st century this is something each one of us needs to address. Removing perfectly good clothes from your wardrobe which you could wear again makes no sense from an environmental point of view. On the other hand, neither does keeping clothes which do not fit you, or which you clearly no longer like and you know you will never wear again. Far better, then, to pass those clothes on to someone who will enjoy them. We all want to look and feel good and we have grown used to being able to buy clothes at relatively low prices. This has given us the mindset that clothes are the ultimate disposable item. This attitude is not sustainable and it does not promote healthy working conditions or a realistic living wage for the people who make them. Not only that: we transport materials and finished clothing all over the world at some considerable cost to the environment. Against these facts we must balance economic realism and that fact that so many people obtain their livelihood from the fashion industry.

GUIDANCE FROM THE OTHER SIDE

For our part, we can become more aware and ask more questions about the origin of the clothes we wear and wear those clothes for longer. If we are honest about what we truly need, we shall be encouraged to buy less. That being the case, maybe we can afford to spend a little more on each item. We can also consider buying second-hand online and from more local sources. Another way to prolong the life of the clothes which we have is to remodel them creatively. If we feel bored with an item then can we make it into something else? The expression "make do and mend" was popular during the Second World War, but it is just as relevant today. We can save buttons and other trimmings and just have fun with the clothing that we have. Good clothing should not end up in landfill – this must stop. Some of the clothing we wear today purports to look like natural fibre but often it contains a high proportion of man-made material that will never rot. So good reason to check labels and be careful what we are buying in the first place. When decluttering clothes, find a good home for those clothes which you know that you will not wear and pass them on, or alternatively consider giving them new life by making a few changes yourself.

If you understand who you are, you can make your own decisions about how many items you need in your wardrobe and know why each item is there. This is very much a personal decision and it is more important to get to the point of "enough" rather than to remove swathes of clothes and then find you want to buy more later. If you live in a country with a very changeable climate then it makes sense to keep clothes for all seasons. Far better to keep those clothes for many years, even if they are worn just a few times a year, than to remove them and be cold and wet.

Clothes should be treated with respect. Not just respect for how we look when we wear them but respect for the work and resources which have gone into making them. Because we have learned to treat clothes as disposable, we throw them out as soon as they look a little dated or if we notice that even a very minor repair is needed. It is not so very difficult to repair fabric and prolong the life of our clothes. If we are prepared to get a little creative, then we can jazz up old items and give them a new look. This is not a concept that is popular today, but if we travel back 50 years or more this practice was commonplace then. Clothes can be a lot of fun for many people – and we need fun in our lives! This is just about switching the focus from new to re-use, from fast fashion to long-term sustainability, but still feeling the joy when we wear the things that we love.

The Marie Kondo approach is to declutter clothing first and she suggests putting every item of clothing you own in a pile on your bed. Personally, I would just pull out of the wardrobe every item of clothing in a particular category at one time. Start with trousers, say, and then shirts/tops, etc. There is a limit to how many pairs of jeans you need, or how many t-shirts. The number/type depends on your lifestyle, but often doing this exercise highlights just how many items you have of a particular type. Marie Kondo suggests picking up each item individually and asking if that item sparks joy. It is a lovely idea and does make you think about which clothes make you feel happy and which don't. By the time you get to your tenth pair of socks you might be having difficulty thinking whether the pink pair or the blue pair spark more joy than the green ones, but I have used this method myself, together with Kondo's folding methods, and I do think her ideas are really helpful, even if they are not always so easy to maintain.

The additional issue with decluttering clothing is that many of us have clothing in "aspirational sizes". If you have ever bought anything and think, "This is a bit tight, but I'll slim down" you will know what I mean! Inevitably the item becomes tighter and is confined to the back of the wardrobe. But just as with other items, clothing that you cannot currently fit into represents an alternative you that you aspire to become (one day). I am much better at decluttering clothes which are too big once I have slimmed down than I am with clothes which are too small when I have put on weight! Throwing out the small sizes seems like an admission that I will never be slim again (which I may not be, but getting rid of them means I have to come to terms with that, or do something about it). Like many of us, I am still work in progress.

Sentimental Items
It can be difficult to part with things which provoke memories of childhood, or of people who are no longer here. It is often very difficult to justify why you want to keep a chipped jug that your granny kept on her kitchen windowsill; even more difficult if you have ever tried to justify it to anyone else. To you it means the world, but to others it looks like an old-fashioned jug with a big chip on it. Make sure that your sentimental items evoke positive sentiments and get rid of anything that reminds you of sad times in your life. Even the sentimental items should spark joy and happiness.

It can help to identify the things that are kept purely for joyful sentimental reasons and give yourself permission to keep them by placing them in a special memory box. I would suggest putting a limit on the space you allocate for this and don't use it as an excuse to hold onto everything that has ever been inherited or given to you. The sentimental items which you retain should feel very special and consequently there should not be too many of them. I have allocated three plastic boxes in my attic space and these boxes contain things such a special toy that evokes happy memories of my children's childhood; cards from my children when they were young; some copper ornaments my grandfather made; and other special things I love. I might bring a few of them out into the rest of the house from time to time, just so I can appreciate them, but on the whole they remain in the boxes so I can have that trip down memory lane whenever I want. I have every intention of revisiting those memory boxes over time and will probably trim down the collection further. The real memories are in my heart and the items are there just to help the recall. Realistically, a photograph on my phone would do the same job, but the point is that the clutter is currently managed and I know exactly where to go to find the items I want to retrieve. They are not occupying my head space by my moving them around the house and wondering what to do with them. When I go, they will not mean a thing to anyone else and will inevitably end up at a charity shop.

Useful Someday
This is the banana skin of your decluttering efforts! "Useful someday" is a dangerous category because it gives you permission to hold on to things until they are no longer useful to anyone. Even if they are hidden out of sight, anything that you own is connected to you by an invisible energetic thread until you break the thread through your intention to part with that item. It doesn't matter if these things are in a shed at the bottom of the garden or in your attic space, the principle is the same. So please think about this, if you keep your grandad's wheelchair in the loft space – just in case it will be useful someday; are you not then setting an intention that it WILL be useful someday, and that someone will need it? Far better to pass it on so it can be used immediately by some who really does need it now. If we accept that like energies attract, why keep something like this?

One of the main reasons why people keep things which might be useful someday is because they are worried that there will be a point in the future when they will unable to buy what they need, or at the very least not be able to locate the item again and they will be lacking in some way. Once again you are setting a negative intention about your future life and this time, setting an expectation of being poor. If we can accept that keeping things "just in case" sets in place an intention, that you have an expectation that a particular scenario may play out, please make sure that the scenario is a pleasant one! I have honestly heard of perfectly healthy people keeping wheelchairs and walking frames, previously used by elderly relatives "just in case" they need them themselves at some future point. What sort of message of intent does that course of action promote? That one day you will need them, of course! Not storing these items will not guarantee that you will not need a walking frame or a wheelchair in later life, but why not give them away/sell them to someone who needs one now, and not bring your energy down every time you look at them? Fashions change and things generally do not improve the longer you keep them. The likelihood is that whatever you have kept like that may not suit your future needs anyway.

It may be worthwhile keeping an extra kettle or an iron, in case the one you have suddenly stops working, but if you have so much stuff that you cannot find things when you need them, you end up having to buy them again anyway. Far better to think what you need now and make some balanced decisions about keeping one or two extra items stored away where you know exactly where to find them.

If we have a large enough home, or even if we don't, it is inevitable that someone in the family or one of your friends will ask you to store items for them. They might be in between homes themselves, or travelling overseas, and have collections, etc. which they cannot take with them for whatever reason, and you have little choice but to store someone else's possessions. Offspring have a habit of doing this and I have to smile when I hear that a son or daughter is moving out of the family home, as both they and/or their stuff have a habit of finding their way back at some point – if only briefly. As a parent, most of us would not have things any other way, but whatever the reasoning, storing other people's things can still feel like physical and mental clutter. All you can do is to ask the person concerned to regularly review what they have stored with you to make sure you are not storing things they no longer need or want. If some time has passed and their lives have moved on, too, you could find yourself storing things for years which they will eventually collect and just take to the tip. If all else fails, and if it is in any way practical to do so, it is worth putting a time limit on this and say that everything must be collected by a certain point in the future, and stick to it. If you have dealt with your clutter and you are housing other people's, you will not exactly feel joyful every time you look at it. Even if the items are stored out of sight (in a loft, for example), you are ultimately responsible for those items. If you are sensitive, I believe that you can actually "feel" clutter – or rather the energy of it – and if you have a lot of stuff around you it can become overwhelming, whether it is yours or anyone else's.

Making Decisions

It is not always so easy to make decisions about what to keep and what to pass on. It can be far too overwhelming to attempt to clear your entire home in one go, too. You could just start with one drawer and work from there, if necessary. As with the "aspirational sizing" of clothes in my wardrobe, some of these decisions are easier than others. The reason Marie Kondo suggests that the way to start decluttering is by gathering all your clothes together and putting them on the bed is because when you see all your clothes in one place it can be quite shocking. It is not until everything is brought together that many people even realise how many individual items they have. Even very rich people only need so many suits, so many coats and so many jeans. How many in each category depends on whether they spend most of their days in suits or jeans. However rich they are, there are still only 365 days in a year in which to wear all this stuff.

Deciding which of your personal belongings to remove from your life must be your decision, and yours alone, unless of course that item is jointly owned and then you must respect another's wishes. If you know someone whom you think of as a hoarder and intend "going in and sorting them out" – please think again. People hoard things for many reasons and their home can represent their state of mind. Often it can be a response to loss in other areas of their lives, so please tread carefully. Just create your own sacred space and be there for people with help and advice, but only if they request it.

For your own part, if you are not sure what to get rid of, you can create a "holding zone". Some things will be easy to part with, others you will know that you definitely want to keep, but quite a few things fall into the middle ground. Using the idea of the memory boxes might help for all those little bits and pieces which do not exactly fit anywhere, but there will be other things which were either relatively expensive to buy or you are genuinely not sure about. If you can separate those out and put them somewhere, whether in an attic or a wardrobe, label them up "to be reviewed". As you become more confident with the decluttering process, you will find that the whole thing gets easier and less stuff ends up in the holding zone. It is worth giving yourself time to make decisions. You can review the items you have placed there in a few months' time, or even after a couple of years if necessary. This is all about creating that sacred space around your body that serves you well. There is absolutely nothing to be achieved by making life more difficult or stressful while you are trying to reach certain decisions.

When thinking about the physical stuff, it is worth pointing out if you don't get round to clearing out your stuff then someone else will have to do it – eventually. I have had to clear out a few homes over the years and it is a very sad and depressing process. You try desperately hard to respect the decease person's wishes and respect their privacy, but in the end it was their stuff and it needs to be cleared. Depending on the circumstances, there often isn't the luxury of being able to take weeks over the process, either. The best time to get on top of your own clutter is when you are fit and able to do so. I want to make things as easy as possible for the people who have the job of sorting things out after I go.

The other point to consider is that one of the main reasons people move home is because they feel they have outgrown their previous place. Wanting more bedrooms for an expanding family is one thing but spending a great deal of money to get extra storage space for "stuff" is mad if you don't really need all your things in the first place. The time to declutter is before you move because the process will make you much more aware of what future space you actually need.

People
This might seem a strange category to include here, but if we are clearing our physical space then we need to think carefully about the people whom we allow to come into it. We are clearing spaces of negative things so that we can fill that space with a higher vibrational frequency.

We often instinctively know which friends raise our frequency and which ones lower it; which friends and family uplift us each time we talk to them, raise our energy, and from whom we come away feeling joy at the interaction. Not everyone can be up all the time and when going through troubled times, friends and family need us more than ever and we can be there for support even if we come away feeling drained. We know that they would do the same for us and we would not have things any other way. However, we often know people who meet with us or call us just to "off-load". There is no reciprocal arrangement or positive energy exchange at any time and you get to the stage when you dread the phone ringing. The term "energy vampire" has been used to describe such people and if you know any, you might feel this is an appropriate term. Not only can some people suck all the energy out of you, but you occasionally come across people who are so negative and unpleasant that their energy feels very heavy.

Depending on your relationship and responsibilities, it is acceptable to cut someone free if they fall into this category and if you feel there is absolutely nothing you can do to help them. Always be kind and offer alternative suggestions about places or people who can help them and always send the person positive energy. Interestingly, as you make the decision or set the intention to cut someone free, you may find that they contact you much less or not at all. On some level, their soul knows that you can no longer be used in this way and it can be a learning process on both sides.

Just as an aside note here, when we are talking to anyone – either remotely or face to face – we can send them positive healing energy just by setting the intention to do so. If we give our energy freely and with love then it doesn't deplete us in the same way as when someone takes it. This can be a difficult concept to grasp and even more difficult to accept, but everything we think and feel has its own energy just as much as the things we say and do. This is why we must always aim to be kind, compassionate and understanding when thinking about others, but we must also treat ourselves in exactly the same way. The next chapter discusses this concept in more detail when talking about Control Dramas.

Friends and family who treat us like a doormat to be walked over must not be assisted in this endeavour by us lying down on the floor for them to do just that. We must give ourselves the same respect that we give others. If anyone is treating you in this way, and especially if you love them, start the process of opening up a dialogue to explain how they make you feel. You are doing both of you a great disservice if you fail to do this and allow the situation to continue. If they are thoughtless towards you then they are probably treating others the same way – if not now then in the future. The time to have the conversation is when you are not feeling too emotional about the situation, so that you can explain your case clearly. No one likes to have their failings pointed out to them, but communication is the key to all successful relationships, as are trust and kindness.

There may be times when no amount of communication on your side achieves the desired effect. If that is the case you can take a step back, and if it is not possible to remove yourself then you can take the decision to remove some of your energy from the situation so that the thoughtlessness does not cause you so much harm. If this is the case, continue to send the person lots of loving energy and healing as often as you can. You may be very surprised at just how powerful this can be and the situation may resolve itself.

After the Decluttering
You should now be in a position (or on your way to one) where you are feeling a degree of peace in your surroundings. There isn't too much clutter vying for your attention and you have more space around you than previously. The question now is what to do next.

We all have a different idea about what constitutes "clean": what I might class as an acceptable level could fall far short of what you may be happy with, and vice versa. There is also the issue of how many people are living in a space and how many people are willing to spend time cleaning it. It is however much easier to clean if you are not storing piles of things on the floor, or have very large pieces of furniture which are impossible to move. Keep this in mind as you are planning your new space. A few pretty storage boxes can transform a space, as can repositioning large pieces of furniture. Try and look at your home with fresh eyes and think where improvements can be made. Just because something has always been where it is since you moved in, it is not necessarily the best place for it now. So the next step is a deep clean of the space whilst thinking about how to make the job easier in future.

The aim here is to allow energy to flow freely around your home and to ensure that there are no areas where energy can get stuck. If all you have done is to pile things around the edges of the room then dust will collect and it will be much more effort to clean everything.

Uplifting Your Home

Just as we need positive energy to flow around our body, we need it to be able to flow around our homes too. If energy gets stuck we can sense it on a very subtle level, and depending where it is, it can have an impact on our daily lives. As a guide, if your home is very easy to clean and you can move things without too much effort, there is a good chance that energy is flowing. If you walk into a room and you knock your leg on a stool and have to embark on an assault course to get to the other side, there is a good chance that energy is not flowing as freely as it should. The aim is to have just the right amount of furniture in your rooms. If you have been serious about decluttering your belongings, you will find that you do not need so much furniture for storage. Space is beautiful! It really is. In modern day living, and especially in terms of real estate, space has a monetary value, too. Why waste that space by filling it with furniture to store stuff you don't need?

As you become more sensitive to your soul body, you start to become much more sensitive about the energy flow within your home. It is possible to adjust and balance that flow of energy so that it can enhance your life. If you have adopted the decluttering mindset and decided which items bring you joy and uplift your spirits when you look at them, you can then move on to ensuring that the placement of those items enhances your life as well.

Feng Shui

With the literal translation of "wind water", feng shui is the ancient Chinese art of placement that was first used 3,000 years ago (Karen Kingston, 1996). It was originally used to determine the most auspicious sites for ancestral tombs, as it was believed that the correct placement would have a positive effect on the lives of descendants. It was later used to establish the position of palaces and important government buildings; feng shui practitioners train for many years to understand this vast subject, which has various "schools" with some contrasting and sometimes contradictory rules.

GUIDANCE FROM THE OTHER SIDE

Most of us do not have the luxury these days of choosing a building plot based on feng shui rules, but wherever we live we can adopt some of the principles to improve our lives. At a very basic level, feng shui promotes the idea that our home is divided into nine separate sections and each section represents a different area of our lives. This is an enormous subject and was a particularly popular topic in the United States and the United Kingdom the early 1990s. Feng shui fell out of favour in China, but was still practised in Hong Kong and many buildings are orientated according to feng shui principles. For further detailed information, publications by Karen Kingston, Sarah Shurety and Simon Brown are a very good place to look: there is more information in the bibliography. Feng shui is a fascinating subject and you can employ the services of a trained and experienced feng shui expert if you wish to explore the subject further.

Home Energy Flow
What I am going to offer here is not feng shui but a much simpler approach that acknowledges the importance of a soft and flowing path of energy through your home. It aims to align the energy of your house or apartment with things you want to attract to you. Your home, however humble, should be your sanctuary – your safe place. It should represent your soul spirit as it is now, and how it aspires to be. If you are comfortable and feel joyfully inspired in your surroundings then you can live the spirit within and find further happiness.

The cleaning and the decluttering must come first; that is non-negotiable. If you are only part way through this process, then just apply this checklist to the individual rooms that you have prepared. The idea here is to work with what you have; having decluttered, there is absolutely no suggestion that you should go out and buy more! If the building that you are living in or the furniture that you have does not appear ideal then you work with it and apply various "cures" to rectify the situation. These could be as simple as adding a mirror, or placing a crystal or a plant in a particular position to soften the effects of a sharp corner. This is all about a clear soft flow of energy throughout your home and rectifying areas where energy is getting slowed down or stuck, or where sharp pointy objects are channelling harsh energy towards you. Even on a subconscious level, we react to everything we see, feel and hear so it makes sense to consider how we use our home to ensure that our energy is as harmonious as possible.

First, go outside or to the external entrance to your home and really look at it. What do you see? This is the area that greets you and everyone else. This is your face to the world and it should feel joyful and welcoming. Is the door clean? Can the number of your building be clearly seen? Is there any rubbish stored near the doorway? Where are your bins? Try and look at your home through the eyes of anyone who visits. If you have a dead pot plant or hanging basket by your doorway, what is that saying to others? It suggests that you do not care enough to remove it and the dried-up display has the potential to lower your spirits when you get home. Far better to remove the pots out of sight and ensure that the entrance to your home looks fresh and uplifting.

As you enter your home, what is the first thing that you see? Are there shoes and coats strewn around overtaking the space and narrowing the entrance as you walk in? Has your hallway become a dumping ground for things which you plan to get rid of? Can you even fully open the door? Once past your front door, this is the first sight that welcomes you, your family and visitors. Does this area uplift you or bring your spirits down? If it uplifts you because the first thing you see is a beautiful crystal or a shelf/table containing much-adored objects then this sets the tone for much of what happens once you are inside. This is your sacred sanctuary. It is your safe haven and your home should feel as though it is enveloping you with love and welcoming you as you enter.

Go through all the rooms in your house in the same way and ask yourself some key questions as you go round. Are the windows clean and letting in as much light as possible? Can I fully open the door to the room? Can I move freely in the room without knocking my legs on sharp corners? Am I storing any items in piles on the floor? If you are then your energy drops each time you look down at them. Also, they are less easy to move when cleaning which makes the job so much more effort. Are small everyday essential items stored in pretty boxes so that they are easy to clean round as well? Am I displaying only beautiful things which lift my spirits?

Think, too, about the overall placement of furniture. Look at each room with fresh eyes. Is your furniture positioned in the best place? Is it conducive to conversation and family life? If all the furniture in your living room is facing the TV, is there anywhere else for the family to gather and just talk? If not, is it possible to create an area that will encourage quiet conversation? Good communication is essential for harmonious family life, so it makes sense to design spaces where the family feels comfortable coming together.

For whatever reason, we sometimes end up with furniture that is not of our choosing, or even through our choosing we end up with something that just doesn't work in the space. In the past I have resisted passing on pieces of inherited furniture which were either too big, too impractical or just not needed anymore, all because they held memories for me of people no longer here. It is so easy to think that we are giving away the memories when we give away the items, but of course this is not the case. We will still retain the memory and the energy of all the happy family gatherings held around a particular table long after that table is creating happy memories for someone else. It might be possible to swap what you have for something else, or otherwise part with it on one of the many local free exchange websites.

When looking at bedrooms, think about where beds are positioned in relation to bathrooms, windows and doors. Although a bed can look very attractive backing on to a window, it is not always the position most conducive to sound sleep. You are more likely to suffer from temperature extremes and it could make you more aware of outside noise than if the bed was placed against a solid wall. The same can be said of a bed backing onto a bathroom wall if that is used during the night. Ideally the bed should give a clear view of the doorway so that you can see who is entering the room when you are in bed. It helps if there is space either side of the bed to place two equally sized bedside tables if two people are sharing and these should contain the minimum number of items for restful sleep. Your bedroom is your absolute inner sanctum and it should be the place where you feel most comfortable. It is the last place you see at night and the first place you see in the morning. What do your eyes settle on as you lie in bed? Your eyes should be met by something that inspires you, rather than something that brings your energy down, so think about where you place dirty linen baskets, for example, and put them out of sight if possible.

Your bedroom should reflect the energy of the activities which take place in it. For all of us that includes sleeping but if you want to encourage romantic activity – and many people will – then make the space feel romantic. Decorate the room with romantic images and avoid pictures of lone females or males, especially if you are looking for someone to share your bedroom with. Having to move 20 soft cute and cuddly toys before you get into bed might not be setting the right scene!

Most of this is about common sense, but it is all too easy not to consciously notice these things and just accept things as they are. Not everyone lives in a rectangular building with perfectly straight walls and standard shaped rooms. Sometimes we are left with sharp corners that point into a room or deep beams that sit overhead. Where possible, think about how energy works its way around these things and see if the corner can be softened by placing a green leafy plant in front of it. Alternatively, if possible, move beds or sofas slightly away from overhead beams so that you are not sitting directly underneath them. Owing to the size of our homes it is not always possible to avoid these things, but try to develop a sensitivity to the space and feel if things are in the right place. If something feels "off" then trust your judgement and move it somewhere else.

Maintenance

When you have decluttered surplus items and passed them on either by selling them or giving them away; when you have rearranged your rooms and reacquainted yourself with lots of lovely extra space; when you have uplifted and enhanced the energetic flow so that everything in your home feels right to you – what's next? Maintenance is next, because you should have reached the point of "enough".

Some people adopt a "one in, one out" philosophy, others go on to realise that they need, or want to declutter more, but what you don't want to do at this point is to let your home slip back by buying more things. We are creatures of habit and nature abhors a vacuum so you might find that things "find you" now that you have more space. This could be someone in the family wanting you to store their things for them, it could be someone who lives with you who hasn't quite bought into the decluttering concept to the same extent as you have and has decided that the newly-found space needs filling. It could be you falling back into old habits and buying things you don't really need. Whatever the challenges, please be aware that these things can happen immediately after decluttering.

Shopping is a major recreational activity and if we are truly intending to buy less then we must question whether we need to find a different activity to take its place. That's not to say we don't have other hobbies, far from it, but shopping is a nice cosy activity to indulge in and if we are changing our behaviour then we need to approach it in a different way. I am very conscious of the decline of the high street and the need to generate income in the economy. If we can foster the idea of re-use and respect when buying things, we can support local businesses which have sustainability at their heart. We can continue to buy consumable items and now have time to take much more care over their purchase. If we still want to buy beautiful objects then if they are supporting an artist or local crafts person, or they are pre-loved, all well and good. We just need to be sure that we are buying things which we love and will continue to love for a very long time. Rather than buying objects for friends, let us consider buying them experiences. A shared pottery class, for example; maybe a simple shared picnic in the countryside. Can you honestly remember what your best friend bought you for your last three birthdays? Experiences will be remembered far better than things and they sustain friendships as well as the environment. Moving forward we need to be much more creative about how we spend our money and our lives. While connecting to our soul selves we can come to conclusions about what is enough for us personally. Don't fret if you know people who own just 30 items of clothing and three pieces of furniture in total. That is their reality, not yours. We are all on a journey and their ability to declutter to a greater level than yours does not make them a better or more spiritual person. We have all been dealt a different set of cards and it is what we do with them that counts.

The Body as a Sacred Space
Having created a sacred physical space within which to connect, we now need to bring our attention to the immediate soul packaging – our bodies. As I have said before, the spirit world has absolutely no interest in your physical appearance, but it is helpful to have a body that serves the soul's purpose in terms of allowing energy to move freely and easily around it, and to ensure where possible that your movements are free-flowing.

Food
Your body will respond as best it can to whatever your mind thinks it is capable of. The opposite may be true as well. We have all heard the

expression "we are what we eat", but it is also true to say that "we are what we think". Never is this as true as when you put the two phrases together. Our true essence knows exactly what foods we should eat and in what quantity. Unfortunately, we have learnt to override this guidance and largely ignore it altogether. If you are a person who has always thought of food as fuel and nothing else, and have always maintained a healthy weight, then you will find that this next section does not apply to you.

Experience has taught me that I have a strong interest in food and that I use food for more than fuel for the body. How on earth did this happen? I also believe that I can "think myself fat". In other words, when I look back at pictures of my young self, I was clearly not fat at all. At the time, I was comparing myself with people of a completely different body shape to mine and against an ideal image that was unrealistic in the extreme. What I have learnt since is that by constantly reinforcing the fact that I was unhappy with my weight, I created the conditions to put on extra weight. The mind tends to give us what we want and expect, and constant reinforcement makes the connection much stronger. Of course, if I had only ever eaten very healthy food in small quantities then I would not have created the cycle in the first place! Having spent a lifetime thinking in this way, it takes a great deal of effort to move away and choose to do something different. If we are talking about decluttering our immediate surroundings to create sacred space then we really do need to address our thoughts about our body as a sacred space too. This is not just in terms of fuelling the body with food but also providing the body with the opportunity for constant movement so that energy can move more freely.

So how do we approach this in a more spiritual way? How can we honour our beautiful soul by providing just the right physical body for it to thrive? Food is sustenance, but it can also be a comfort. Eating was designed to be a pleasurable way to get fuel into the body. If it had been painful or unpleasant then people would not have decided to do it and they would not have survived. What is happening now is that food has moved away from serving purely as fuel and has become a pleasurable activity that is often linked to reward, as well as sustenance and excess, and anything else we want to associate it with. We use it in ways it was never intended for. In richer societies we have 24-hour access to foods which are not always ideal or healthy and we now have difficulty in making judgements about what we should or should not eat and drink. We feel that we deserve to reward ourselves with alcohol and certain foods, or that we need the comfort and the high which certain foods and drinks can give us. In other words, we have exalted the importance of food in our society and we keep moving further and further away from what it was intended to do.

If you compare for a moment how we treat our bodies to how we might treat a car, we do not "overfill" a car – and yet we are very happy to do that to our body. For one thing, it is not safe or desirable to have fuel dripping out of the tank on to the floor. It costs too much money to do that and the car doesn't go any better for it. In fact, if you fill your car with substandard fuel you wouldn't expect it to work very well at all. You would expect it to break down and to cause you all sorts of problems. You don't tell your car that because you overfilled it last week it will have to work just the same on very little fuel this week, and if you haven't filled it to the required amount with good quality fuel, you don't get angry with it when it needs a bit more. As the driver, you accept that to keep your car working and reliable, you must do what is best for it.

This does not apply to everyone, of course. Not everyone lacks self-control when it comes to food. They understand the food as fuel concept and honour their bodies through the selection of the freshest and healthiest foods in minimum quantities. They never hear the call of the bar of chocolate languishing in the fridge, or that last piece of cake which refuses to leave their attention until it has been consumed. Very restrictive diets are clearly not the answer and can actually be harmful to the body.

Neither is it helpful to think in terms of "I have eaten x, y and z and have therefore failed". We need to forgive ourselves and find workable long term natural solutions that can be maintained indefinitely.

The body has been designed to react to hunger. It is a useful reminder that your body needs more fuel, in the same way that the fuel gauge reminds you to fill up the car. If you ignore the fuel gauge then the car will continue to run for a little while; it may complain by slowing down, or spluttering, and then will eventually stop. The same can be said of the body.

The difference between the two is that the car cannot (yet) take itself to the fuel station and select its fuel, decide for itself how much to put in, or even what price to pay and what grade to use. This is where the analogy ends. People do have free will and they use it to control the food fuel that they take into their bodies. On one level this is a very positive thing to be able to do. If you see food that is putrid and covered in maggots then, however hungry you might be, you can exercise your free will not to eat something that you think may be harmful. If you are lucky enough to live somewhere where food and clean water are in plentiful supply, and within your economic means, you will be making decisions constantly about what to put into your body.

We are social creatures, so gathering together for food provides a social focus. In times past, it also ensured that whatever food there was would be shared equally within the group. The elderly needed less, the workers needed more, but everyone's basic fuel requirements were met in a very egalitarian way.

It is of course very different now and people's relationship with food has changed. The focus should be on using food to enable your physical body to work at optimum health for as long as its earthly life will allow it. I do not believe that we can control all the illnesses that we sustain in this life, but if through our actions we can promote and encourage a healthier body, we may just be able to give it a fighting chance when facing illness. If you want to walk a spiritual path, ideally you want a body that will assist you in that aim.

Movement

Something that was made to very clear to me in different meditations is the importance of moving and stretching the body. It makes a great deal of sense when you think about it. The aim is for energy to move freely: when we do not exercise or stretch our bodies they become "set" and eventually become unable to move properly. This must have an impact on the way energy flows, not to mention the various aches and pains which accompany a lack of movement.

Fortunately, for a large part of my life, I have enjoyed yoga both by attending classes and practising at home. However, I must be honest and say that I have also gone for long periods where I have not done any practice at all. Life has a habit of getting in the way of our best intentions. When you have a busy job and there are not enough hours in the day to do everything and you feel tired, that is when exercise is unlikely to happen. I have certainly been in that position and had to bring myself back after some long gaps to try to regain my previous level of movement. When I am exercising, especially when doing yoga, I feel more alive.

Whatever your form of exercise it doesn't really matter, as long as you are stretching and moving on a regular basis. Yoga particularly appeals to me (and there are many different types), but that is just my personal preference.

Everywhere we look, there is lots of advice about how to get thinner, fitter, healthier and generally be a "better" version of ourselves. We need to "think ourselves healthy" and know that we can achieve our own personal optimal health and fitness without getting fanatical about it. We all have access to a large amount of information about what constitutes a healthy diet and I believe it is possible to eat healthily and reset that inner guidance.

There is a mountain of help and information around, and of course certain medical conditions require specific approaches.

It is worth looking at your overall health and fitness and, if you feel it is necessary, trying to unpick why you over-eat or under-eat, and how much stress and emotion plays a part. Knowledge is power, and by being honest and examining these behaviours one by one, you get to understand much more about yourself and what drives you. Notice things about your body and how it may be reacting. Trust yourself to know and understand what constitutes a healthy life and notice what you are feeling and experiencing when you deviate from that. Ask yourself if you are using food or alcohol to dull feelings of sadness or stress. Notice when you make unhealthy choices: what is going on at the time? Are you too busy or too tired to care at that point? Above all, do not be too hard on yourself. The aim is to achieve optimum health. Happiness is much more important so take a broad view and just do your best.

If you do feel it is necessary during your meditations, you can ask for the strength to deal with any particular issues you may have which will result in a healthier you. You may be surprised at the effect that has on strengthening resolve.

Working With Inner Guidance – Looking for the Signposts
If at this point we are spending time connecting with our soul, we have looked carefully at everything around us and we have ensured that our home is a sacred sanctuary that will nurture us, we are now ready to harness further guidance about how we can live the best life possible.

Obtaining that guidance can take different forms. We can sit down with pen and paper in hand (or sit at a laptop) and just see what we are guided to write. We can pose a question and just listen to see if an answer appears. Or we can just write about what has been happening in our lives and see if our writing shows any clarity at the end. Sometimes we are guided without even being aware of it; we just need to make some space in our lives and be available. This involves finding a place of peace, trying to clear our minds of other thoughts and just being open to listen to what may or may not come to us.

If all this sounds a bit too nebulous then if we have a problem to solve or a decision to take, we can just sit quietly and write different options on a piece of paper, and then write down the advantages and disadvantages of each option. The actual act of writing prompts the mind to look at problems from different points of view. If we have our various pieces of paper and still do not know what to do, we can just give the problem over to our self soul and ask for a sign as to what the best option might be.

Seeing the Signs
Signs can take different forms and may just result in inner knowledge, rather than a theatrical gesture. We can also become too fixed on what we accept to be a sign. Some people look for feathers as a sign from other worldly sources either that a loved one is with them or that they are on the right track with their thinking. For me, seeing feathers represents a cat (normally mine) who has been rather too successful at chasing birds; my heart sinks at this point and during the warmer months it isn't such an unusual occurrence. I have received signs, however, and they have not always been what I was expecting or could have ever anticipated. They are, of course, even more surprising if someone else witnesses them.

A few years ago I had been reading a good deal about past lives and trying to make sense of my own experiences. As anyone involved in spiritual work will tell you, belief is fine but there are times when you need some clear validation that you are connecting with spirit and not suffering from an overactive imagination. Wanting some form of proof now and again is healthy in my opinion and although I have had a connection with the spirit world all my life, this has not stopped me questioning every new piece of information that comes my way. I have an enquiring mind, but I think it is important to run everything past your higher self to see if what you are being told feels right to you. On one such occasion I had been reading an excellent book by David Wells about Past Lives (Wells 2008) and it prompted me to record information about my own past life memories. This was not the first time I had written about my past lives, but I had always "left the door open" to include other possibilities as to why I might be able to recount these stories, such as connecting with another form of intelligence, or just plain "making it up". Having said that, by this point I had been able to obtain some firm validation of at least one life, but it still did not stop me questioning what I had just read. I am a Medium – and just being able to admit this has taken me a long time. I have had difficulty accepting that I am talking to people who have departed, or indeed reside purely in the spirit world, and on this particular morning my latest read had prompted me to ask for some clear and irrefutable proof that I wasn't a complete fruit-cake.

It was a cold but clear and sunny Saturday morning in very early January and my husband Chris and I decided to take a drive into the countryside and include a short walk. Just before we left, I asked for a sign to confirm that everything that I thought about the spirit world and the validity of my past life experiences was correct. As I sat in the car, I heard the words, "Tell him that you have asked for a sign". I duly passed on this information, but hearing his wife come out with odd other-worldly statements barely registered anymore and besides, Chris was much more interested in leaving the house and going out for the day. As we didn't have a fixed idea where we were going, it was more a case of leaving the house to see where we ended up. After a few miles, Chris stopped the car at a lay-by next to a field in Northamptonshire. There was a monument commemorating the Battle of Naseby at the top of the hill, which could be reached from a footpath running alongside the field. The Battle of Naseby was an important and decisive battle during the English Civil War. We had never been before, but Chris said he had often wanted to walk up to the monument and look at it. As I stepped out of the car, I instinctively looked down at the muddy ground for a feather – or anything – that might constitute a sign. Nothing. I largely forgot about signs at that point and started walking up the hill. There was no one else about and it was all very rural and peaceful.

When we reached the monument, there was information on a board describing the battle. The Battle of Naseby was fought on 14 June 1645. It was fought between a Parliamentary army of approximately 15,000 men led by Oliver Cromwell and a Royalist army of approximately 12,000 led by Prince Rupert, who represented Charles I. Approximately 1,000 Royalist soldiers died on that day, in addition to 150 Parliamentarians. Needless to say, this was a very bloody battle and one which eventually determined the final outcome of the Civil War: the defeat of the Royalist army and success for the Parliamentarians. The information in these surroundings describes the position of the various forces and also mentions the advance of the King's cavalry, led by Prince Rupert on a white horse. As we were standing taking in the view, we could both suddenly hear what can only be described as something resembling musket fire! Chris was desperately looking for a rational explanation as the sounds continued. What was interesting was that the sounds were not coming from one point but from several different points across the field. Chris eventually insisted that the noises must be coming from some sort of mechanical bird scarer (?). In January? He then proceeded to look around, somewhat desperately, for confirmation of what seemed to me like an improbable theory. We stood there for several minutes and the sounds continued. It was as though we were listening to the audio of a play – and not at a low volume either. Chris then noticed a white horse on the ridge in the far distance. I noticed it too. Clearly someone was on the horse, but we couldn't make out from that distance any distinguishing features about what they might be wearing. At this point Chris was keen to get back down the hill and into the car, so that he could see where the horse and rider joined the road. In his interpretation, there was no way that the horse and rider were imaginary and therefore they would have to reach the road at some point and could clearly be seen "in the flesh". During the short walk back down the hill I did start to think that this might be my sign – and a very dramatic one at that.

We reached the car, and Chris wasted no time in driving along to where the mystery horseperson had to join the road. There was nothing. This freaked him out more than the noises in the field! Sceptics could argue that we imagined the whole scene. That the noises could have had several rational explanations and that through the power of suggestion we recreated the vision of the person on the horse (or that we just missed them as they exited the road). I would not blame them for that, except for the fact that we both witnessed exactly the same thing at the same time. I accepted this as the sign I had asked for. It was particularly relevant as my question had related to reincarnation and past lives. What better example could I have been given? Chris struggled to find an explanation but agreed that we had witnessed something very unusual.

The follow-up to this story is that Chris was so incredulous about what we had experienced that he suggested we go back two years later to the day to see if the same thing would happen again. I went along with this, but honestly wasn't expecting anything. I had received my sign and I was happy with that. Why on earth should we expect anything else? So we both approached our second visit with very low expectations, and sure enough, we got to the top of the hill next to the monument and there were no noises to be heard. After a few minutes, for some reason (I have no idea why) I decided to say out loud to the field, "So you have no noises for us today, then?" Immediately, the musket-like noises started again. This time they were much quieter but definitely there and they did not start until I asked the question! By this point Chris didn't need any more convincing that we had experienced some other-worldly phenomenon on both occasions, although there was no sign of the person on horseback this time. This was a turning-point for Chris, to the extent that he decided to listen more carefully when his wife came out with something "weird". I should probably mention that a couple of years after the second occurrence we went back to the same spot again. This time there was nothing, not even at my request.

Signs can also take the form of that uncomfortable feeling when something just doesn't feel quite right. This has happened to me a great many times over the years and I have turned down promising jobs when they felt wrong. If I wake up in the morning with a concern that I didn't have before I went to bed, then I take even more notice. I believe that our soul, in connection with the spirit world, can contact us through dreams which we may not be conscious of at the point of waking. It can be as simple as bringing to mind that there is something we have forgotten to do, or it can be a niggling feeling that we should or should not do something. It is not always easy to explain or justify, but you could call it knowing that something isn't quite right.

On the whole I have always listened to these niggling feelings and acted on them, but there have been occasions when my logical mind has stood in the way and I have attempted to dispel those inner guidance feelings and do the opposite. When this happens, the warnings just get stronger; I think I have finally learned my lesson.

We tend to keep cars for a very long time and so when we buy another one it is quite a big deal. We were looking for our next vehicle and made a list of all the features we would like. There was no question of us buying a new one, so finding it involved looking at online advertisements and narrowing down the selection to somewhere within a 30 to 35-mile radius. After a bit of searching we located one and went to view it. It was perfect in every respect except the price; it had all the features on our list and it looked great. The part-exchange on our own vehicle was much less than we hoped, but for the car of our dreams we went away to see if we could stretch to the extra. We went back to look a second time and could not get this car out of our heads. Unfortunately, though, there was something niggling away at me and I woke up on several mornings with the words, "This car is not for you" in my head. It wasn't just the price, it was more than that. It was a feeling that we shouldn't buy it, which was odd because on paper it was almost perfect. Taking notice of "the feeling" we walked away, but every few days we kept thinking about the car and wondering if we should go for it; this dilemma went on for 39 days! Finally, with more repairs needed on our old car, we said – this is silly, we haven't found anything better in all this time, let's go for it. We finally made this decision late on a Friday afternoon and decided to set off early on Saturday morning to seal the deal.

We left home in perfect sunshine and commenced the 30-mile drive to the garage. We were around two thirds of the way there when suddenly torrential rain came down and we found ourselves in a storm. It was still early, as we intended to arrive as soon as the garage opened and we had left home without anything to eat, so we decided to pull off the road and have breakfast first to give the rain time to stop, as it would be safer to drive. After all, who would buy a car in a major storm anyway?! We sat down in the restaurant, ordered and looked out of the window; the sun was shining and there was no sign of any rain! Where did it go? By then we were already seated and rather hungry, so we carried on with our plans to have breakfast first. We didn't waste any time and as soon as we had eaten we got back on our way. As we arrived at the garage, we could see "our car" from the back and confidently approached the sales office to buy it. We were met with, "Sorry – I sold that car 20 minutes ago". Just 20 minutes! If we hadn't been in that storm and stopped for breakfast then we would have got there first. The universe did not want us to buy that car! It had been for sale for the previous 11 weeks, and yet it was sold 20 minutes before we got there. I should have listened.

GUIDANCE FROM THE OTHER SIDE

The follow-up to this story is that exactly a week later, we found a similar but cheaper car. This car was much further away but around 20 miles from where our son lived, so he said he would meet us at the garage and make sure we were not buying the wrong thing. He had never been there before, either, but it turned out that the salesman's sister had been at my son's wedding, and his parents lived in the same road as our son's boss. It certainly felt as though we were finally in the right place. So far it has been a great car, too, and we love it. I am not convinced that the other car was wrong as such, but maybe it was right for someone else. In other words, as I was told: "This car is not for you".

The final example of a sign that I am going to share with you was when we were thinking about moving closer to our family. We had been looking for a long time and couldn't really see what we were looking for. Nothing was quite right, despite doing a very large amount of research and looking in a wide area. In the end we decided that we should put our house on the market, try to get a buyer and then look again, as we would be bound to find somewhere nearer to our family then. Why we would think that when nothing felt right up to that point I am not sure, but that is what we did. To make our current house more saleable, we decided to make some changes to the bedroom. We were halfway through these changes when I went upstairs to take a look and was suddenly met with the most awful feeling. It is very difficult to describe, but I switched from happy to sad in an instant and felt as though I had been shaken. The feeling I had was one of absolute dread! I knew instantly what it was. It would be so wrong of us to move to a new house now. I went downstairs to attempt to explain all this to Chris, but he admitted that something had been niggling away at him, too, so he was only too happy that I had come to the same decision. Within a matter of minutes we had abandoned many, many months of planning and had gone from absolutely going to move to not going anywhere and being very happy about it. It was as though I had been ignoring all the subtle signs and in the end the spirit world had to take me by the scruff of the neck and give me a good shake (in energetic terms, anyway).

This also turned out to be the right decision. Our daughter was one of the people we were moving to be closer to and she ended up getting another job and moving to a different part of the country; where we currently live is actually closer. We would have been trying to move during the Covid 19 lockdown, and after spending so much more time in the house we realised that we already had everything we could possibly want in a house, and that for the foreseeable future we needed to stay put.

Not all signs are as dramatic as that, of course. Answers to our questions can come via dreams or even through snippets of conversation heard while passing someone in the street. I honestly believe that our soul wants the very best for us, and that the spirit world wants us to learn to appreciate the signs and use them to help us make the right decisions.

Coincidences

There are so many key life events which seem to come about because of coincidence. Finding the house that is just right for us; even meeting our life partner. When we are on the right track, things seem to fall effortlessly into place; and other times, despite everything looking right on paper, things just don't work out.

I have written down my future visions for decades and on my wish list many years ago, when the children were small, was a house move. We wanted more space, and that room to dance, but also to be near a good school. I had a clear vision and to help it along, years before, I had cut a picture from a magazine of my "dream home" and attached to the fridge in the kitchen so I could look at it; I also listed all the features it would have. Friends and family would see it and were too polite to laugh at the time, but probably did on the way home. I should point out that at the time, the dream was quite unrealistic – not least from a financial point of view. Anyway, several years later our circumstances started to change and a house move looked like a more realistic option.

When we were looking it was at a time when it was advisable to try to sell your current home before looking for another. We sold our home very quickly, but had already missed out on a couple to buy which seemed to be perfect. One of the main criteria was to find somewhere near to a good school, but it also had to feel right. Eventually, we thought we had found our dream home: it was just perfect for us, and looked exactly like the picture on the fridge. This had to be it, surely? We made our offer only to be outbid and, not wishing to get into a bidding war, which was common at the time, we had to walk away. Since we already had a buyer for our house, we had to look for one to buy before they walked away. Eventually, we found one that my husband loved, and on paper it certainly seemed to fit the bill. I wanted to make it work (it didn't look like the picture, but I didn't consider that). As property was going so quickly, we decided to shake hands on the deal at the second viewing. Unfortunately, the moment I took the seller's hand, I knew something was wrong. This was not the house for us – but how on earth was I going to tell my dear husband and family, who were all very excited at the prospect of moving? The following day I had to speak up because I knew we were making a mistake. Me and my "funny feelings" about things have been a bit of a bane to my family over the years, but it is very interesting how they tend to respect and act on them regardless. Having turned down a house that should have been perfect, I then had the problem of finding one which felt right, especially as our existing house had a buyer. I found another house and although I wasn't that keen, I decided to call the estate agent to arrange a viewing. Coincidentally, although it was a different type of house, it was next door to the one where we had been outbid and was being offered by the same estate agent. Whilst on the phone, for some reason I started to tell them that we had missed out on the first property that happened to be next door to the one I was now enquiring about. As luck would have it, the people who had outbid us had just backed out that morning and the seller was on another phone to the estate agent to arrange for the house to be re-advertised. Fortunately, the agent I was talking to told me all this. So, the seller of our dream house was on one call to the estate agents at the exactly the same time that I was calling about viewing another house, and within minutes of the first buyer dropping out. Coincidence?! If I had not made the call that morning, the house would have been re-advertised and owing to the state of the housing market at the time, we would probably have not got it. My funny feeling had paid off.

So, was this a coincidence or divine intervention? When friends and family saw where were moving to, they could not believe that it looked the same as the picture of the house that had been stuck on our fridge for the previous couple of years. The picture of course was accompanied by a list of all the features our new house should have. Everything was right except for one thing – the price! We had to pay a bit more, but on the day that we moved I received a phone call moments before the telephone was disconnected to say that I had been offered a new job. In my mind, we were moving to exactly where we were supposed to be.

Many people have stories like this, especially relating to property. Relationships are often another area where coincidence plays a part. You can look back and think, "Why did I go to that particular party?"; "What would have happened if I hadn't walked into that shop just when I did?" I actually believe that coincidences sometimes help to put us in the right place at the right time and some of the most important relationships can come about as a result of seemingly random events. It can also be a reinforcement that we are in the right place when we find that a person we have just met knows someone we do. The universe finds lots of ways to offer guidance if we just look.

GUIDANCE FROM THE OTHER SIDE

Listening to Your Dreams

The spirit world sometimes attempts to contact us through dreams. Not all dreams are messages, of course, and sometimes our brains are just ordering and making sense of things we have seen or done during the day. I do believe, however, that somewhere in that ordering we can still find some guidance if we give ourselves time to think.

For the most part, I can only bring to mind the occasional dream when I wake up, and many of those can dissipate quickly upon waking. I have very occasionally had mini premonition dreams; the most notable for me was "seeing" the garden of where we now live, long before we had any intention of moving to the area (the district was told to me as well in the dream). It wasn't an exact replica of the garden in terms of a perfect photograph but the garden had some very specific features and issues present which enabled me to recognise it easily. I also occasionally have dreams that I do believe represent direct contact from the spirit world in the form of a deceased relative "talking" to me. These feel very different to me and the memory of those dreams stays with me long after waking. On those occasions, I pay specific attention to what happened. When I say "talking" to me in a dream, I never actually hear the words or see their mouth move – it is more like telepathy.

Finally, probably the most guidance I obtain from dreams is when I wake up "knowing" something. This will be something I had not thought about during the day, or for many days/weeks prior. But I can wake up realising that I have forgotten something, or have a feeling that a particular course of action is not advisable; these are the messages that I have learned to act on.

Everyone is different and the way you obtain guidance from dreams may be very different to me. These are just examples, but in Resources (Section G) there is a template that you might like to use to record dreams which seem worth noting.

GUIDANCE FROM THE OTHER SIDE

False Signs

Not everything in life is a sign! You cannot abandon common sense and logic – the two have to work together. I would not start a relationship with someone I had randomly met just because he/she knew some of the people I did. I wouldn't see it as a sign if the feeling wasn't there. There are times, though, when you can pass your fate over to the universe and say something like, "I like this person, we keep meeting accidentally – if I am supposed to be with this person then the universe will make it happen". You can then stop worrying about it, because if it is meant to be then it will happen.

We often look for signs when someone has died, and at that time we can want a sign so badly that we are willing to take almost anything as a sign that a loved one is with us. Just because a butterfly has flown in through an open window and is trying to get out does not necessarily mean that your departed relative has come to visit you. They may have, but it could just be a butterfly that has flown in by mistake. There used to be a robin that appeared whenever we were doing any work in the garden and we used to say that it was my father who had come to check up that we were doing everything right. On one occasion the robin followed us about so much that I was tempted to think this way, but realistically, I honestly think it was just a robin looking out for worms that might have come up to the surface as we were digging the ground. That is not to say that I do not think it is possible or likely that departed spirits use birds and butterflies, etc. to get your attention. When you are working so much with the spirit world, it is very important to keep a grip on reality. As you work more with your soul, you are going to become much more sensitive to how you feel, and to what does and does not feel right. Your soul is there to guide you in positive ways, but it absolutely does not tell you what to do. If you ever start to hear voices which are telling you to do specific things, they are not coming from your true soul or a spirit source that is there for your highest good. This will never happen. The spirit world respects the fact that we have free will and it wants us to use it. It wants us to learn from our experiences. At best, you will get a feel for which direction to go in or an opportunity to look at things from different viewpoints. The signs are for reinforcement and must never replace a research-based approach to taking all the important decisions in your life.

Deciding what is a sign may depend on context. I entered an early online competition to win a reading with world-renowned Medium Gordon Smith that would take place in a few months' time in London. I was very busy at work at the time of entering and decided to check my diary before entering the competition to make sure I was free. I am not particularly successful at winning competitions and certainly would not normally check dates, but as I pressed "send" I got that feeling again that my efforts might not be for nothing. I was still very surprised and delighted when I found out I had won. The whole experience was amazing and finally gave me the absolute proof I needed that everything I had thought was true. On the way to the venue to receive my reading, I almost stepped on a beautiful butterfly that was just lying on the pavement on a busy London street. This was in January! You do not expect to see a butterfly on the pavement in January. I thought it was odd at the time and was very glad that I saw it in time, before I contributed to its demise. Part of my wonderful reading included a message for someone else. You will read later that I do not make a habit of passing on messages intended for others and this was only one of two times that I did so. As I shall explain later, passing on unsolicited messages rarely goes well, but I thought to mention to the person concerned that I had seen the butterfly on the way to the reading. This was the one bit of the message that she took as evidence, as she always associated her mother with butterflies. So, context can be the key.

GUIDANCE FROM THE OTHER SIDE

Chapter 3 Summary: Harnessing Inner Guidance

Identifying what your personal version of "enough" means

- Clearing physical and mental space:
    - Notice your surroundings and decide how they make you feel
    - Do all your belongings uplift you, or do they bring your energy down?
    - Do you own too many things, including items which you don't like or need?

- Dealing with the process of decluttering:
    - It is important to analyse why you are holding on to certain types of clutter
    - Do any of the things you are keeping represent an aspirational version of yourself?
    - Some types of clutter will be easier to clear than others
    - How to deal with items which have sentimental value and those you think might be "useful someday"
    - How to make the right decisions, including about the people you have around you

- After decluttering, uplift your home:
    - Feng shui and home energy flow concepts to make your home your own private sanctuary
    - How to keep up the good work

- The body as a sacred space:
    - Optimal health through food and movement

GUIDANCE FROM THE OTHER SIDE

- Working with the inner guidance without signs:
    - Reinforcement that we are on the track or wrong track can take many forms
    - Identifying coincidences
    - Not everything is a sign

CHAPTER 4
OVERCOMING BARRIERS TO PROGRESS

If you have been following the recommendations, at this point you should be well aware of how physical belongings can affect your sanctuary space and even your head space. You are probably already thinking about decluttering and have a fairly clear vision about what you want in your life. You may even be thinking about making other changes, to ensure that energy flows through your body and you are in the best physical shape possible. Great! What could possibly go wrong?

If only life was as easy as making a decision to do something and then seamlessly carrying it out. We all know people who are incredibly focused and seem to achieve their aims with "seemingly little effort". People who give up smoking overnight, or decide to train for a marathon and complete it. I suspect that for them, making those changes was far from easy. When approaching a new way of doing things that is a bit outside the normal for us, we can often put up our own barriers before we even get started. If we try to take on too much in one go we can get overwhelmed. Some people want to take on an all or nothing approach, others want to start small and work up. Many of us probably fall between the two approaches – I know I do. My default pattern is to start off well on a particular regime and then around three to six months in, many of my good intentions fall by the wayside. For me, it is as though I must prove to myself (not to anyone else) that I can do something, and three to six months in I appear to have given myself the necessary proof. Unfortunately, three to six months is not long enough to achieve the overall aim. So around a year later I am back where I started, with slightly less motivation than the last time because I am convinced the same thing will happen again! What have I learned from all this? I have learned that I put up myriad barriers to create some sort of warped logic that will give me "permission" to fall back into old habits.

What I have had to do is to unpick all that warped logic and try to work out where it was all coming from and what I could do about it. Understanding yourself and forgiving yourself is part of the way of solving the problem. We are not living in a perfect world and there is nothing to be achieved by metaphorically beating yourself up for not matching an ideal version of yourself. The answer is to acknowledge setbacks as well as successes and, figuratively speaking, "get back on the horse as quickly as possible"!

Each time we pick up where we left off, we get a little bit better at overcoming resistance. The more we understand about ourselves, the more we can get ready for the dip in motivation and develop strategies to prepare for it. In effect, we are all works in progress. Some issues will always be issues for us, other things which others may find overwhelming can quite honestly be a doddle.

Identifying Your Barriers To Success

When sitting surrounded by that light-filled bubble discussed in Chapter One, you can eventually start to benefit from the guidance on offer. There may be clarity when sitting like this, and that is what you are aiming for. It is not as though you are likely to hear a booming voice in your ear that sets you straight: it is more about an acceptance of your foibles and a sense of how to make things better. If you know, like me, that you can start off with good intentions and then fall by the wayside, understanding more about yourself and why that happens can put you back on track. As a process, a good place to start is to try to understand what preconceived ideas we have buried in our heads about why we are not doing something.

One obvious reason is that we think our efforts will be fruitless. If we don't actually believe deep down that anything we do will make a difference, then we are setting up a barrier and telling our soul self that we know that what we are hoping for will definitely not happen. And if we put that energy out there, then that is what we will get back. If we can accept that it might work for others but not for us personally, and we cannot see ourselves in the role, how can we achieve that aim? The expression, "If you think you can or you think you can't – you are right" expresses this perfectly. If we are energy, which of course we are, then we need to align our current energy with what we want more of – not what we want less of. This is why it is so important to speak and affirm your vision for yourself in the present tense, as though it is the reality now.

If you do not believe deep down that you will be able to achieve something then it is very unlikely to happen. Far better to analyse why you think your efforts will be wasted. What qualities do successful people possess which you do not? Why should these things not work for you? Take every one of those objections and work out where they came from. Do these other people, in your opinion, have more time than you? Are they more selfish than you? Do they help people less than you do? By really looking at your objections you can start to break down some of the barriers. You can then start to see where these things come from. Somewhere deep inside you may be associating success in that one area with qualities which you do not want to see in yourself: greed, selfishness, etc. That then gives you an excuse not to take the action, as the end point will result in you being a person whom you do not actually like. The reality is that these preconceived barriers rarely bear any relation to the truth anyway, but it is not until we identify and acknowledge them that we expose them for what they are: false excuses.

In an example from my own experience, there was a great deal of pressure on me at one time, when I first went into teaching, to obtain a Ph.D. I had a young family and everything I knew about writing a dissertation involved long hours at weekends and during the holidays which would take me away from my family. I had no choice but to carry on because at the time I believed that keeping my day job depended on it. I was never going to finish (I had two attempts) because I had preconceived ideas about what doing a Ph.D. involved. In my head, in order to do it, you had to be very selfish and put yourself first – not ideal with a young family, and not something I was prepared to do. Consequently, I did everything else before picking up the dissertation. It was never going to be a successful outcome. The reality, too, is that I know some lovely people who are not in the least bit selfish and who did not deprive their families of any of their time when their children were young, who started at the same time as me, and they completed theirs. So, the premise upon which I made those judgements was fundamentally flawed. One of the other barriers I had created was that I could not actually visualise myself putting "Dr." in front of my name. Titles were not important to me, but beyond that, I was the first in my family to obtain a degree. To go on to get a Ph.D. felt like pie in the sky! Other people who were much clever than me would do those things – not someone like me. In fact, I felt like a complete imposter who should not even have been trying to get a Ph.D. in the first place! My attitude was all wrong. I was sending out "I am not worthy" vibes, "I don't really want or need this" vibes, and at no point did I feel or act like someone who had a Ph.D. or at least was trying to get one! What I know now is that studying for a Ph.D. is all about organisation and discipline. Little and often is the key – not leaving it for weeks until you have done all your ironing. On reflection, if I had wanted to do it enough (rather than feeling that it was forced upon me) I could have made space in my life by, say, getting up an hour and half earlier each day to ensure that the job was done. If I had changed my attitude and aligned my energy to act and feel like someone who already had a Ph.D., rather than acting like someone who didn't really want one, I would probably be writing "Ph.D." after my name on the cover of this book. However, no experience is completely lost and much of what

I learned during those years has helped prepare me for the books which I write today. I cannot emphasize enough that when you think you are not worthy of something coming to you, you send out a message to the universe that you are not.

I have had to overcome other related barriers to success since my Ph.D. experience. One of the most relevant of these was about becoming an author. "Me?" "Really?" "An author? No, you must mean someone else…". I cannot remember how many times I questioned what I was doing. I still do, but the difference now is that I have decided to do it anyway. I am in a much better position to understand where those preconceived objections are coming from. I am not completely sorted, and probably never will be, but I am getting there and I have decided that I might have knowledge or information that is useful to someone else, so I just need to get over myself and get it out there. The interesting thing is that when you take those positive steps, the universe often lends a helping hand.

Barriers to success can sometimes be a little harder to work out. Do you actually want this particular outcome? If not, why not? Is there something in your past that might have some impact on the situation? When it comes to success in financial terms, people sometimes worry that it will alienate them from their present friendship group. To be honest that can sometimes happen, but you would hope that your true friends will always be happy for you. Having more money than your peer group will have an impact on what you talk about and your less well-off friends might feel that if they say how they are struggling it looks as though they are expecting you to jump in and pay for things. Inviting you round to their house might not be a thing they want to do so often if they feel that they do not have the things you have, and they might decide that you are in danger of judging them. So, what is the solution? Do you decide not to be success because it might upset a few people, or do you decide to use any financial success wisely and help people as best you can. If other people cannot handle your success, that is entirely their problem and not yours; having said that, when you love your friends and all the time that you spend together, you may be subconsciously holding back. This can apply to families as well as friends, and to any jealousy within the family that might cause tension. It is very easy for us to make excuses not to do things, so the only important question is: how much do you really want to do it?

Another barrier to doing what you want to do is procrastination. I seem to have procrastination down to a very fine art! Procrastination is the concept that putting something off until a future date will create a set of circumstances that will make that task easier or more favourable to complete (later) than it is today. Circumstances are rarely better at a later date and all that happens is that we build up resistance to completing or even starting the task, until the thing we want to do becomes almost impossible. Procrastination is one of my personal challenges and this book, and others, would have been completed several years earlier if it had not been an issue. As a recovering procrastinator, the best strategy I have is to give myself specific deadlines and work towards those by using time slots. The more you put something off, the less likely you are to want to start it in the first place, which is where the time slots come in. If you tell yourself that you will work on a bit of the task for, say, 30 minutes, the idea is that you build up the time and the frequency until you are back in the flow. We allow ourselves to become distracted because the task appears difficult to us. Very often it turns out to be much easier than we think, but the absurdity of it is that if it seems difficult today, it will still seem difficult tomorrow – only more so. I only mention procrastination here as this has been such an issue for me and something that has delayed my completing things which really were in my soul's best interest.

By recognising the barriers which might be stopping us from doing some of the things we want to do, we are going a long way towards overcoming them.

GUIDANCE FROM THE OTHER SIDE

Energy Exchanges

We are walking energy fields. This section is called energy exchanges because it concentrates on what is happening in our own energy fields and how they have the potential to interact with others. If we can accept that we are all energy, and light-filled energy at that, it is easier to accept that we all have an aura or a light-filled energy field around us that may be perceived by some as containing different colours. Our aura contains information about what has happened and is happening to us, as well as what will potentially happen to us in our immediate or more distant future. I say "potentially", since we all have free will and therefore the ability to overwrite a future potential. Our aura reflects our soul, but it isn't our soul – it is just a representation of the energy field surrounding it. Depending on how we are feeling, aspects of our aura can be picked up by others and read, either intentionally by someone with psychic ability or unintentionally and subconsciously by the people we meet. This is how we can sometimes look at someone and although their physical appearance might suggest the contrary, we may just know instinctively that something is wrong. We can feel it. There is a type of photography called electrophotography, or Kirlian photography, which is capable of capturing coronal discharges, in other words the colours which surround objects, when a photographic plate is connected to a high voltage source. The phenomenon was discovered by Semyon Kirlian in 1939 by accident and this type of photography is often named after him, but it is also often called aura photography (Adobe 2023). Practitioners of this photography offer an explanation about what the various colours of the aura mean. There does not appear to be any strong peer-reviewed academic research to support the fact that this type of photography can detect personality traits, for example, but it is a very interesting phenomenon. There is a school of thought that certain colours in the aura mean certain things, but as with most things metaphysical there rarely is any academic research to support it. One of the reasons is that most academic institutions rely on external funding for much of their research and few universities would be prepared to risk their reputation on something considered by many to be "pseudo-science". If you have an aura photograph taken at different times, the images will almost certainly be different. Our aura represents what is happening to us and that can be represented by the different colours. There are so many things which we do not understand but, as with any activity, try these things but balance it with a good level of common sense. It is sufficient to say that energy can be seen and measured.

As an experiment, and only in a situation where it is safe to do so, try concentrating on someone to see if you can sense colours around them. You may find this easier if you ask them to stand against a white wall. In my experience some people see colours with their eyes wide open and others close their eyes to see if they can sense colours. Whichever method you use, you can record your findings using paper and coloured crayons and then look the colours up online to see if they helped you understand more about that person. You may find out that you start seeing auras when you are watching people perform, or at an event. Again, this is just one method and if you find it difficult to see anything, don't worry about it and try again in a month's time. If it is any consolation, I find this quite a difficult thing to do.

How the Exchange Appears To Work
Our soul, our precious soul, is who we are. It is linked to our aura and the energy field that surrounds our body (auras are not just found around our head but all around our body), but there is a distinction between the two. Our soul is ours and ours alone, and an intrinsic part of us. The reflected energy or aura can interact with others and that energy field can be intertwined with the energy of the people we meet. Other people are not able to interact directly with our own soul while we are in physical

form, but they can interact with the reflected energy from it. This is an important point to note. Whatever may have happened to you in the past, your soul remains whole. Your soul is pure and unadulterated by anything that your physical body may have experienced. It will retain the memory, but not have been wounded by it. Your soul is purity personified; it is the divine part of you. So, whatever you feel your starting-point might be when beginning this spiritual journey, your soul is complete, perfect and safe. As you start to learn how to live the spirit within, you can connect more fully to your soul and benefit from its ability to cleanse your aura, or that reflected energy field surrounding your body, and learn to live a more spiritually aligned life on earth. The spirit world wants us to understand who we are and make this connection. It is very important that we do. It will ease our passage into the next world when the time comes and will help to break the destructive cycles that we unwittingly put ourselves into. Furthermore, when that tipping point of spiritually aligned souls is reached, our earthly lives will be transformed and we will all be able to forge a physical existence that respects our planet and everyone on it.

In the meantime, since we can only change the world one soul at a time, we need to strengthen the communication with that ultimate essence of our being, and learn to recognise where our energy is going and when to give it feely to others.

Whenever we are interested in another human being, even during more casual meetings, our energies reach out to them. The stronger connection we have with the person, the more our energies are shared. Not all of these connections take place in close physical proximity, either: we have extremely powerful senses on so many levels which make reading another's energy possible across even remote connections. All we need is to be able to hear, see or sense the other person and a connection can be made.

If you have ever met someone and known within a few seconds that this person is going to be important in your life, it is possible you are recognising that future potential for you to be together in their aura, when their energy begins to link to yours. If you believe in love at first sight, this may start to explain it. Like attracts like and energy fields which are similar are drawn together. Conversely, this can also explain why we feel uncomfortable when we meet certain people. People can put up barriers, whether they are aware of it or not, so first impressions are not always lasting ones.

By accepting that everything is energy and that we are individual fields of energy which regularly interact with other fields of energy, we need to understand what can happen when energy fields come together.

Control Drama Groups
In this section, all due credit must be given to the author of *The Celestine Prophecy*, James Redfield (1994). I first read *The Celestine Prophecy* and the range of books which followed it in the 1990s. The books can probably best be described as an allegorical account of the author's own spiritual awakening, set in an adventure format where the main character discovers significant spiritual truths whilst undertaking a journey. This adventure parable, as described by Redfield, sets out to discover initially nine insights which underpin our spiritual understanding. Redfield was influenced by Eric Berne's *Games People Play* (1964), but his interpretation has a great deal to offer for anyone interested in energy fields.

Redfield writes about the synchronicity of events and information arriving just at the right time. About how we might think of an old friend and then receive a phone call or bump into them. For me, the most powerful sections of the book refer to what Redfield calls "Control Drama". I felt I must include a section about Control Drama groups in this book because they explain a good deal about how relationships work and what is happening to our energy when we interact with people. According to Redfield, when humans turn their attention to one another, they literally merge their energy fields and pool that energy together. The issue then is who controls the pooled energy. If one person dominates, the other person can feel depleted. The one who dominates can feel a rush of energy and euphoria, as though they have won an invisible battle. We have all felt suddenly off balance when someone has manipulated us into a state of confusion, probably resulting in doubting ourselves completely if we allow this.

The way to step back into your own power is to recognise what is happening during the interactions and give your energy freely, rather than have it taken from you. By giving it freely, it does not deplete you and it frees you from the effects of control by others. Redfield has divided behaviours into the following: Poor Me, Aloof, Interrogators, and Intimidators. In terms of reference, I have offered my own examples where possible and tried to expand the explanations to include some everyday situations which we may all recognise, but I want to acknowledge that I have paraphrased the relevant section in Redfield's *The Celestine Vision* (Redfield J., 1997, Chapter 5, pp. 71-86), where Redfield explains the Control Dramas displayed in *The Celestine Prophecy*. Read below and see if you can identify these behaviours in yourself and others.

The Poor Me

This is playing the victim. Energy is manipulated by adopting a strategy of getting attention through sympathy. Anyone interacting with a Poor Me will be drawn into a conversation that somehow ends up making the other person feel guilty. Depending on the context, a Poor Me will look for sympathy by saying how overworked they are (the implication being that they are doing more than you); that they must complete a task before a particular deadline (implying they cannot do it without your help); and that the overwork is making them ill (that's your fault as well). You don't have to be connected through work or family association to be drawn into the scenario. You could meet an unknown stranger Poor Me while waiting in line who will try and get energy from you by telling you how awful their life is and how this could be their last meal, etc. This is to make you feel guilty that you have more/your life is going better, etc. None of this is to say that we should not be sympathetic and have empathy for people less fortunate than ourselves, but we can give our money, time and energy in an appropriate way that does not deplete us. Within families the role can play out with one family member wanting more than the other can or wants to give. If you phone your nearest or dearest are told "I thought you were dead" or "Oh, so you've decided to call now, have you?", you're talking to a Poor Me.

This behaviour is not necessarily a conscious act – more of a learned behaviour. To the Poor Me, the world (people) has constantly let them down. No one can be relied upon, but they lack the assertiveness to take control of their own life and have learned a pattern of behaviour that makes a bid for sympathy by putting others on a guilt trip. Since we have a habit of getting what we expect, the Poor Me attracts the very situations into their life which perpetuate Poor Me behaviour.

The best way to change this drama pattern is to give your energy freely. Feel that energy leaving your heart and lovingly reaching the other person. Think about whether any of their comments are justified and whether you do need to change your own behaviour. For example, if your phone calls are infrequent and you suspect the Poor Me is lonely, is there anything you can do to help them? If we have done that we might then enter into some sort of dialogue that discusses the behaviour pattern in a loving and constructive way.

The Aloof

Aloofs like a bit of mystery to surround them. So assuming there is no valid reason for them wanting to tell you very little about everyday things, if you find yourself in conversation with someone and can't get a straight answer, you could be dealing with an Aloof. Their behaviour prompts you to request further details in response to their vague statements. For example, in a work context, you may ask someone where they worked before. Many people would give you a couple of sentences such as "I was at company X for ten years" and (if that company was not well known) "They were based in Y and produced Z". Not so for an Aloof. Obtaining the same amount of information could take you weeks and they would very much enjoy the process of watching you trying to find out. A typical Aloof response might be "I've done a lot of things...". You then start to feel a little embarrassed about asking more: "Such as?" "I travelled overseas a lot." No indication of where, why or what they did when they got there, and they have you hooked. Consequently, you are spending your energy wondering about them and as your energy goes wherever you focus, they 'win'.

The way to deal with an Aloof is to send them your energy freely, and then remove your focus away from them. You may find that they come back to you with another intriguing statement to draw you back in, or they may leave it at that. If you have an Aloof in your family it is not so easy to focus away, so after sending them your loving energy you might start a dialogue that demonstrates the behaviour they are exhibiting. All the time send them energy as you do so. It is probably safe to say that many teenagers are susceptible to aloof style behaviour, so further parental enquiry in this case might be not only advisable but essential.

The Interrogator
Whereas the previous two Control Dramas can be described as passive attempts to control energy, the next two are more aggressive. As the name implies, if someone is being interrogated then some sort of blame is being placed at the feet of the interrogatee. The person being interrogated is made to feel incapable of making sound decisions about their own life and is, supposedly, somewhat

inadequate compared to the Interrogator. The Interrogator truly believes that he/she has a better view of the world than most other people, who need to be "put right" to avoid making mistakes. What sets an Interrogator apart from someone who might occasionally want to help is that their behaviour is displayed in a large proportion of their interactions. They will ask questions, subconsciously much of the time, designed to undermine you and make you question yourself. Over time, if you let it, this interrogation can make you lose confidence in your own judgement.

There are obviously times when you may feel very strongly that someone you know is making a terrible mistake and you feel compelled to intervene to help them make a safer decision, but provided this action is not constant and is taken out of a genuine concern and love, rather than in judgement, this does not necessarily make you an Interrogator. The Interrogator will say things like: "I thought about doing that job, but it didn't turn out well and I had years of experience". Subtext: I am much better than you, so what makes you think you can do it? Or "Y's mother does Pilates five times a week, works full time as a corporate lawyer and still has her grandchildren at the weekend". Subtext: what are you doing with your life that makes you so tired at the weekend? Both statements imply inadequacy on the part of the interrogate, even though they are not necessarily phrased as a question. Those feelings of inadequacy translate into a passing of energy to the stronger person – in this case, the Interrogator. This is a win for them and an encouragement for them to continue this behaviour next time they interact.

The Intimidator
Depending on the severity of the behaviour, Intimidators can be extremely dangerous people. If you find yourself in the presence of someone displaying very abusive behaviour, removing yourself will always be the best policy assuming this is possible, of course.

In less extreme cases, Intimidators can still use their behaviour to undermine others and chip away at the confidence of the people being intimidated. We are not looking into the reasons for this learned behaviour here, but it might be as a result of some trauma where learning to be an intimidator was a matter of survival.

The Intimidator controls the energy by creating an intimidating environment around themselves – usually one of fear – by displaying unpredictable outbursts of aggression. The person or people being intimidated then must fully focus all their attention on the Intimidator to try and predict when an outburst is on its way, so that they can try to keep themselves safe. This can play out in a work situation, as well as within the family. If an Intimidator has worked their way up to a position of power within an organisation then their employees work under a banner of constant fear of being called out as incompetent, often in a rather public way. The office bully is an Intimidator, but he/she may not play the same role with everyone. In fact, they can often just single out one particular employee to receive this intimidating treatment, especially if they are not in control of a larger group. They can sometimes switch between Interrogator and Intimidator, to the extent that it may be difficult to call out the behaviour to others.

As difficult as these two more aggressive behaviours may be to handle, the action is the same. By allowing them to Interrogate and Intimidate, you are giving them power that makes them stronger. By sending them loving energy you are depleting their energy and their ability to take energy away from you. You do not have to feel particularly angelic to do this. As difficult as it may be to send loving energy to someone you may view as very unpleasant, your altruistic behaviour will have an immediate impact on how you feel and that will help to reduce the hold they have over you.

As you read these descriptions, you may quickly recall members of your own family who could identify with these roles. You may even identify which role you play! We do not always play the same role of course. We can be a Poor Me with one person and Aloof to another. We can even switch between behaviours with the same person. The important thing is to recognise the behaviour and try to understand what is prompting it. Once you see it for what it is and you send all your loving positive energy towards the other person, you are free from the control. These tend to be learned behaviours and can stem from childhood, but for our purposes we just need to understand that there could be some underlying issues which accompany these actions; as always, tread carefully.

So the method to deal with these behaviours is as follows: first notice it and acknowledge it to yourself; send the person concerned energy from your heart (feel loving energy going from your heart to theirs); when the time is right and you are feeling calm, discuss with them what they do or say, and how that makes you feel.

If in conversation the person you are talking to calls out any behaviour that they find difficult in you, then try not to take the defensive position and calmly consider if they have a point. It is all about learning.

Everyday Dealings With the People We Love
Even though we can communicate via energy exchange invisible to the eye, we must make sure that we do not ignore traditional verbal communication. In many ways it is easier to avoid confrontation than it is to face it. "Anything for a quiet life". Well, no: a lack of communication leads to anything but a quiet life.

If our nearest and dearest constantly do things to hurt and annoy us, we are doing them a great disservice if we don't give them the opportunity to learn and change. The same applies to us, of course. If we keep accepting the hurt, thinking that we need to keep the peace, or assuming that they will not understand, we are putting up a barrier that can over time become impenetrable. Eventually this relationship will have no choice but to break down completely.

GUIDANCE FROM THE OTHER SIDE

(I am not, of course, directing any of these comments to people in relationships where physical or mental abuse is taking place. I urge you to remove yourself from this situation as soon as is practical and seek the help of the many charities which have been set up to assist you. By the time this happens, the relationship is already lost.) I am talking about our everyday dealings with the people we love.

Communication should not always be about correcting the negative, either. It should be about telling those we love how important they are to us. It should be about expressing thanks for all the things they do for us – even those everyday small gestures which make such a difference in our lives. It also needs to be about finding out what the other person wants from life or from your relationship with them, and see if you are both moving in the desired direction. Ask them about their hopes and dreams. Where do they want to be this time next year? Where do they want to be in five years' time, and what do they want their lives to be like then? These should be obvious questions, but if we "think" we know without asking, we might be making the mistake of our lives. How can you truly tell if someone is happy unless you ask them and encourage them to explain themselves? Maybe they are trapped in a job and feel overwhelmed by everything they must do, but put a brave face on things so as not to worry you. It is far better to have those conversations early on, rather than to wait until the situation deteriorates. Find out how people really are and encourage them to talk to you. You may not be able to solve the problem, but at least you will be aware of it and you can work towards a solution together.

It is not being spiritual to constantly bite your lip, to put up and shut up, to mutter under your breath and to complain to everyone except the person involved. That sort of behaviour festers away until resentment sets in and your feelings eat away at you. In the meantime, the source of your annoyance or anger is blissfully unaware that anything is wrong until you either explode or leave – or possibly both. How can that be fair to either of you? Why would you avoid talking and finding out what the other person wants out of life? Why would you let resentment fester and make you bitter when you could have a better understanding from the start?

Ask yourself when you last really talked to your loved ones about what was important in their lives. Are their lives going as they hoped? Did they think that they would be in a different position either physically, financially or career-related at this point? Do they feel as though they are working for nothing, or working constantly for little reward? Do they feel trapped? Ask how you can help them to recover some of what they want. Can you plan more breaks together – if only for a few hours? The years pass by so quickly and no one can afford to put off being happy. We can so easily feel as though we are on a treadmill, a roller coaster even, and cannot afford to get off. Change looks impossible, but there are solutions out there and with love and support things can improve.

So talk. And then talk some more, and talk again and again. The things we want change over time. Not everything remains as important, but other things increase in importance. We are all on a journey, but it should be a happy one. No one should be avoiding going home because they can't face it. Home is your sanctuary and it should be so full of love that it is almost tangible as you walk through the door. We live according to a pattern that we have decided for ourselves. Often this is how our parents or grandparents lived and we follow it without question, but maybe our pattern of living is no longer right for us and we need to effect some changes to make us happy. This isn't about throwing everything away that you already have. It is about working with what you have, talking about how things might be different and changing the journey one small step at a time. No partner should be left wondering what happened. They should not be left wondering what they did wrong. That is unfair.

It does however take both sides of the relationship to engage in talking, and certainly not everyone is prepared to do that. It doesn't matter how much one person is prepared to work at it if the other has no such intention. If one party is set on destructive behaviour then there is often very little you can do but protect yourself.

When the talking has been exhausted, all you can do is to send loving energy to that person and wish them well. You can feel your love travelling towards them and, if necessary, letting them go. Sending out your love is a very powerful act. It helps to release you from any lingering hurt and bitterness and it sets you free.

We are not saints and sending love to someone who has deceived and hurt you beyond measure is no easy task. It will take practice and patience, but when the time is right you can cut the cord of that energy between you. You do this by imagining that there is a rope attaching you to the other person, and that you are holding a large pair of scissors in your hands, and you then cut through the rope until you are no longer connected. A word of warning: do not attempt to do this until you are sure that the relationship is completely over. It is a powerful act and it will release you completely.

Our soul wants us to be happy and to have happy, healthy and loving relationships. We must not assume that we know everything, especially about how other people think. We need to thank the people we care about and tell them what they mean to us. We need to talk and find out what is important to the people we share our lives with and start a dialogue so that they know what is important to us. If we must part, we need to do it with love, because it is the love that sets us free.

Dealing With the Doubters
As American economist Stuart Chase (1888-1985) said, "For those who believe, no proof is necessary. For those who don't believe, no proof is possible" (Goodreads 2023). He may not have been talking specifically about the concept that we are all sacred energy souls having a physical experience, but some people will never accept anything more than the

physical ending of death and we must respect and attempt to understand their views.

During the coronavirus pandemic there were people who believed so strongly that it was not really happening that they felt the need to protest outside hospitals, looking for someone to blame for lockdown. Whatever your personal views about whether the methods employed at the time were necessary or effective, or where the virus originated, to deny that a virus existed when it was killing hundreds of people each day was quite baffling to me. Having their liberties curtailed, and despite being presented with the appalling facts of the disease day after day, the doubters preferred to believe that the risk was exaggerated and was being used as an excuse to control people. They would only have needed to talk to a health care worker and have had some empathy for the souls touched by the disease to question their theory, but rather than that they decided to protest outside hospitals to bring attention to what they believed was a hoax. When you consider how many people were affected by coronavirus, not to mention the illogical theory as to why governments all over the world would conspire in this way, you can appreciate the near-impossible task of getting everyone to believe that we are not just our bodies but also beautiful unique souls who survive after physical death. Essentially, it is a non-starter.

You change the world one soul at a time until there is a paradigm shift, a tipping point of people on this planet who accept that consciousness survives after physical death. By accepting this fact and learning to connect to our soul while we are still in the physical state, we can move society forward to the extent that we are more inclined to work for the common good. If we accept that we are all one, that we are all spiritual beings, any physical differences become irrelevant. Any country of birth, language, sexual orientation or religious belief pales into insignificance against the irrefutable truth that we are all the same, we came from the same source and we are all returning to the same source.

GUIDANCE FROM THE OTHER SIDE

We cannot change other people; we can only change ourselves. We can provide information and assistance, we can answer questions, but beyond that there is absolutely no point whatsoever in attempting to change others through coercion, insistence, persistence or even eccentricity. If people are sufficiently interested in you to ask you about your life philosophy that opens a door to talk to them about what you believe. Not even your nearest and dearest may take the trouble to really ask you what you believe. If they do and they do not agree with your views, that doesn't mean that they don't love you: it just means that they find the subject uncomfortable and would rather not think about it. Just because you find it life-enhancing to know that energy survives after physical death, they may feel extremely threatened by this and, at the very least, this thought could keep them awake at night. Respond to questions in an appropriate, loving and simple way. Always leave the door open for future conversations – but their beliefs are not your problem!

Not verbally expressing the full extent of our beliefs until invited to do so can be a very difficult thing for us to accept. I am not suggesting for a minute that we deny any part of ourselves; we must be always authentic and true to ourselves. What I am saying is that we must accept that we cannot change others and that, in some societies, expressing the views expounded in this book is extremely undesirable, even unsafe.

Even in countries where we believe there to be free speech, informal social networks can ridicule ideas such as these and any mediumship demonstration must legally be described as for "entertainment purposes only". It is important to appreciate and understand how threatened people are when you challenge their long-held beliefs. In many cases it is much easier to believe that when you die that is it, no further come-back and it's all over. They refuse to accept any sort of spirit communication, as that would open the possibility that not only their beliefs but some of their education is in question. Scientists, particularly, can be very reluctant to accept these beliefs and like to use the words "pseudo-science", "woo-woo" or whatever phrase is current to dismiss these ideas as absolute rubbish. The typical reaction is that someone who believes this is completely deluded and has no concept of mainstream science. At worst, they might think you are out to con people, steal their money and prey on the sensitive feelings of the bereaved.

So please tread carefully with love and respect when discussing all things other-worldly. Many of my friends are Psychics and Mediums, so from time to time I receive messages from them which are destined for people I know who do not share the same spiritual beliefs. As the messages have been given to me indirectly, I must take on trust that what they have told me is correct, so I ask for a personal sign that I should pass on this information – but I can still get this wrong! I have twice in the past taken a chance and passed on messages to people known to me, if I thought the person concerned could accept it. To be honest, neither occasion ended particularly well. I knew both parties did not share the same beliefs, but hoped that the fact their loved one had made contact would override that. Whether what I told them confused and upset them, or whether the original message provided enough evidence I shall never know, but on balance I shall not be doing it again. If someone walks into a spiritualist church or some other demonstration of mediumship then you can be more certain that they are reasonably open to receive a message from a loved one in spirit. However well-honed you believe your mediumistic or psychic ability to be, you should never walk up to someone you do not know and deliver a message from the spirit world. There is absolutely no way that you can possibly understand how that person will react to that message once you have left them, and it is unfair to leave them in this way. I know this is contrary to a few TV personalities who do just that, even when out shopping or eating at a restaurant, but giving unsolicited messages from the spirit world is not a good idea, however certain you may be that the message needs to be passed on. There are quite a few Mediums and Psychics who may disagree with me on this point, from the understanding that we work first and foremost for the spirit world, but our objective is to leave people in a better place than when we found them. They should be elated and uplifted and much happier after receiving a message, and if they didn't ask for or particularly want a message this will not always be the case.

If your beliefs are challenged and you do find yourself the subject of abuse or ridicule, I think the only course of action is to avoid the continuation of hostility by not getting involved in any attempt at justification or confrontation, and apologise for expressing views in their presence which they are unhappy about; then remove yourself as quickly as possible. You are not apologising for your views, just for the fact that expressing your views is making them unhappy. It is not denying who you are. It is an act of self-preservation and there are plenty of people around who do share these views and who are very happy to talk to someone else who is as "weird" as they are.

Although there are people at the opposite end of the scale when it comes to beliefs, there are also a great many people who occupy the middle ground. They leave the door open to the idea that consciousness survives death and are interested in hearing about unusual experiences. They approach everything with a healthy degree of scepticism, but they may choose to believe if sufficient evidence comes their way. I am also of the firm belief that very many people have psychic and mediumistic ability, whether they are aware of it or not. For those who do, some are not ready to develop those skills and that is their choice.

Self-Sabotage

Just as we have other people to doubt us, some of our biggest critics are ourselves! There is a fine line between self-analysis and constantly telling ourselves that we cannot do things. As discussed in a previous section, our preconceived beliefs can limit what we believe it is possible for us to achieve. Often, when things are going well, we can self-sabotage our efforts in the strangest ways. Not always consciously of course, but why, when we supposedly want things, do we allow this to happen? Everyone is different, but one reason may be fear. Stepping out of our comfort zone is scary for many people. Doing what we have always done and knowing all the possible outcomes can feel like a very safe place to be.

Whatever your latent fears, it is well worth being honest with yourself and identifying what they are. Most of my earlier ones were to do with not being available for my family and not being the sort of parent I wanted to be. On the one hand, I think that was as much about knowing myself as anything. Parenthood was the most important job in my mind and trying to do it well while holding down a full-time stressful job and studying for that Ph.D. became a constant battle in my head – hence sabotaging the Ph.D. for the sake of having no regrets about the family. I did not *deliberately* or at the time *knowingly* sabotage the Ph.D., but that was in effect what happened. Not only that, I probably just "got by" as a mother, but my children are a constant source of joy and have turned out very well, and still want to spend time with me, so on reflection the balance was probably about right.

On the one hand it is easy to see that within self-sabotage there can be a choice about how you want to spend your time or, equally, a type of fear about feeling overwhelmed. On the other hand, it may be more about the fear involved in becoming someone whom you do not immediately recognise. Stepping out of your comfort zone will inevitably bring you more into the public eye and if your default position is to keep your head down and blend into the background this can be extremely difficult, too. It is impossible these days to start any sort of business without having to engage on social media. Clearly how comfortable you are with that will depend on where you are in your life and how good you are with technology. I still cannot understand why standing up in front of a class of students held less fear than posting things about myself on Instagram. I know it is illogical, but the latter feels like showing off to me – something which as a child I was constantly being told not to do! If it is all about the product or your work (such as on a website), that seems fine to me, but you cannot grow followers doing that and everyone wants to know the human backstory. The idea of stepping up and saying, "Look at me" fills me with dread, but the reality is that if I didn't engage even a little bit with that process, I would not sell a single book. Subsequently, the information about the spirit world that I believe it is very important for everyone to know would never leave my computer. I would not be fulfilling what I believe, a contract I made a very long time ago – many lifetimes, even. So I have had to address this fear, but I will be honest and say that I am far from over it. Like so many things and like so many people, I am "work in progress".

So please go back and look at your vision for yourself and decide if getting everything that you have asked for will hold any fear for you. Ask yourself truly what it feels like to live that life every day and think about how you will overcome any fear surrounding it. This is not an invitation to give up on your dreams: it is an invitation to address any issues which might arise so that you do not create any scenarios which may take you further and further away from what you hope.

Just one final point. Fear can have a habit of wearing us down and making us ill. It can sometimes be the illness itself that becomes the saboteur. The whole point about learning to listen to that subtle soul guidance is that we cease to be bobbing about on a rocky sea and understand more about ourselves, especially our soul body.

GUIDANCE FROM THE OTHER SIDE

Chapter 4 Summary: Overcoming Barriers to Progress

- Identifying your personal barriers to success:
    - Does an obvious pattern emerge?
    - What are your preconceived ideas about successful people?
    - How will the changes you plan affect your friends and family?
    - Is procrastination an issue for you?

- Energy exchanges:
    - We have an energy field around our body (our aura), which can be seen
    - This energy can interact with the energy field of others
    - We can recognise energy exchange via Control Drama groups

- Control Drama groups:
    - The Poor Me; the Aloof; the Interrogator; the Intimidator
    - We need to recognise the behaviour pattern and send loving energy
    - Talk calmly through the behaviour and ask yourself what you have to learn
    - Keep communication lines open for the people you love

- How to deal with the doubters and responding with love

CHAPTER 5
STEPPING INTO YOUR TRUE POWER

By connecting to your true essence, you are able to live the spirit within and harness your true power, rather than completely identifying with just the physical body. The soul is about love, light and higher vibrational qualities. As you make this connection you benefit from greater clarity in all things. It can take a little while, not everything happens immediately, but you should find yourself feeling more joyful and finding pleasure in the little things.

Walking in Nature
Walking amongst nature is one of the most powerful things you can do to strengthen this connection. Seeing plants, green fields, animals in their natural habitat, you are aligning yourself with their energy.

One particularly clear channelled message that has come from Battrick, the spirit communicator of *Answers from the Other Side*, talks about the healing quality of nature. What follows in this chapter draws very heavily on additional channelled messages received on this subject over several months; much of it is reproduced verbatim, exactly as it was received, but the rest is paraphrased. To distinguish between me talking from my own experience and the communication I received directly from the spirit world, I have made a distinction below (the channelled material is in italics).

When you are in the countryside your soul connects with every living thing in that vista and is enhanced by it. You must get out into nature, as it is the best way to connect to the soul; it is easy to lose your connection if you stay inside. You need to feel the breath of fresh air, the smell of grass and feel the wind and rain on your face and the sun on your head. This is how your soul energy is enhanced – without it your soul lacks lustre. Walk by water, walk under trees every day if you can, regardless of the weather.

Battrick emphasized the importance of stretching and always trying to walk gracefully. Lumbering around and sitting in a chair too long is not good for anyone. Not everyone can, but when there is the opportunity, you should be outside in nature. He suggests that when people are too sick to go outside, nature in the form of plants and flowers should be brought to them, but if doing so, make sure that the plants and flowers are changed regularly because after a while they will lack lustre too. If nothing else is possible, a representation of nature in the form of a picture, or by playing natural sounds such as bird song, is beneficial.

When we walk in nature we must observe it – really look at it. Parks and gardens are good for this purpose. Touch the plants and trees; walk on the grass and connect with nature at a very deep level. There is a collective energy in a park or any public space that is frequented by lots of people and which is surrounded by nature. The energy in these places is "peaked". The plants and trees interact with different energetic fields all day for as long as the place is visited. The wildlife picks up on the energy of the diverse range of people who have been there. Not just on that day but the whole time that the place has been popular. The result of all this energetic interaction is that the surrounding "air", as you might want to call it, is knowledgeable and connected to a wide network of other people and places. Although the people (souls) have left the park and travelled to other parks and places, the original park and all the subsequent parks create an energetic memory field connection with everywhere that those people go to, both in physical and spiritual form.

As people have been visiting open places in groups for a very long time, and our world is now very densely populated, these parks – especially – are connected to everywhere else on earth and in the solar system (if any of the souls which visited the park are now residing there). It makes these well-frequented places more connected in energetic form than everywhere else. Therefore, if you have a place that has been visited for many hundreds or thousands of years by people from all over the world, you can see how these sites are particularly well-connected. Once an energetic pattern has been established, energy is pulled in from everywhere. This can help to heal a place that might have had something happen there which you would consider "unpleasant", as the energy is diluted by the positive energy it is connected with.

Walking amongst nature is a very powerful thing for people (souls). It can reconnect them to something larger than the concerns in their own lives. We urge you to visit more of these places and to understand what we mean. The best places are those which retain a lot of nature within them; rather than concrete man-made structures which you can still find in a well-visited place. The reason is because it is the trees and the plants which retain the imprint of the visitors. Trees are a filter, so they transmute negative feelings and energies into something more positive. This is a one-way filter, so you cannot be brought down in your energy or connect to something negative, unless it has happened very recently, before the energetic transformation has taken place.

To return to the bliss state (or rather to get there, as this is not something your planet remembers or has any recollection of), more people need to walk amongst trees and plants, and they need to do it much more frequently.

Gardens are useful too and certainly help, and that includes the healthy plant on your desk, but the difference is that within your own home boundary there is less chance to mix with all souls and so the learning is reduced. Still valuable, but not so well connected.

Julie: So, what might you pick up by visiting these places?

Not so much "pick up" as imbue. It is a two-way process; please do remember that. It is an energetic mingling that has mutual benefit.

It works through the melding of the energy fields. You cannot expect to leave a park and know how to do a complicated mathematical equation if you have not had an advanced maths lesson in your life, but you can expect some clarity in other areas of your life. To get that, you need to release your tensions and focus on the area around you. To look at the plants and feel the trees. To notice the dappled sunlight filtering through the trees or the crisp leaves beneath your feet. You also must do this for a while before you get the full benefits.

It is true that even just looking at a green space can start a healing process, but if you want to be "healed" (and this is at soul rather than physical level, although the two are connected) then you need to make walking amongst nature a big part of your life.

Not everyone can do this and some of your parks are not considered to be safe, but where possible walk in nature-filled areas as often as you can. A rebalancing of modern life can take place.

It is not just in parks, gardens and woods – woods being the most beneficial if they are well visited – but also moors and coastlines. Anywhere that nature is apparent. In a more open space the energy is faster and can be harsher and it is continually refreshed. A different space, a different method or process, but the outcomes are very similar. Walking in nature brings spirits back to their bliss state. Not immediately and not always in one lifetime, but it is very important to the spirit and not indulged in enough by people on earth. Many say they are "too busy" or "too worried" or "too old/infirm", or even too alone, but we are here to tell you that even small steps are important. Work at connecting more with nature and visiting open and natural spaces as often as you would consider visiting your supermarkets or your retail stores.

If people spent as much time outdoors and in nature as they do in centrally heated or air-conditioned shops, their souls would be much happier.

There are benefits on many levels. Not least because of the connectivity of all things. Parks are a place for thinking. It is when amongst nature and your brain is resting that your soul can solve a problem. This is not going to be on the first visit, or even the second, but when the body and brain realises it is amongst nature and can relax, it is in the perfect place for the soul to connect to the invisible network that stems from there and make connections which it would not be able to make while sitting at a desk. There needs to be stillness, a type of peace for this to happen. It is not instant or guaranteed, but humans need to make the space for it to happen.

Not enough people are walking in nature. Many parks are small and do not encourage people to linger, but this needs to change. The more people use them, the more they will enjoy them and relax.

It is the combination of the nature of the plants and trees, etc. and the nature of the soul that reaps the benefits. In these areas the body and soul are more relaxed. Although a supermarket is a public space and many people from various places visit it, when you are there you are concentrating on what you are going to buy, how much money you have and what bargains you can pick up. The brain is busy at these times and the products on sale – most of them anyway – do not have a live energetic field. Walking with nature is very different to that. You should try it.

Julie: Yes, I must. I suppose like many other people, when I have some spare time, I head for the shops or to a coffee shop, rather than walking in nature. It sounds crazy to admit that now but it is the case. There is normally something to do or get, and then by the time you have done that you head back home, telling yourself that the weather is not just right for a walk, or any another excuse.

The weather does not matter. Rain or sun, it does not matter. Hot or cold, it does not matter other, than making sure that the body is comfortable so that the brain can relax. With suitable clothing, whatever that may be, and with regular visits to the same or different places, the body and then the brain know that this is a time to relax but be awake.

Many people sit in a chair or on a sofa to play a computer game or watch TV and say that they are "relaxing". Sometimes, depending on the game or the film, their brains may be still but their body is still paying attention to various stimuli – even if that is just signals that it is time to go and make a drink or open the next can. This is a very different experience to walking in nature. Walking in and amongst nature, what we might call "walking with nature", is a mutual energy exchange and not a one-way passive or almost passive exchange. Focus does not have to be on one area, so people will see things differently and their soul (if not their body and brain as well) will learn to love the experience whatever the weather.

You do not need to make this a chore (a "job" to do, to the exclusion of things you would like to do). It needs to be inherent in your life. It needs to be your salvation and something you are doing because you want to and you know it makes you feel good.

It will take a while for many people to find space in their lives to do this but once they do, they will not go back. They will miss the connection and want to recreate it as quickly as they can.

Julie: Are any places better than others to walk?

In the first instance, anywhere you can get to! Not everyone can travel far to the ideal place. Start with your local park – a short stroll. Then build up from there. Visit places when you leave your city or visit friends. Make walking with nature a big part of your life. You should try it. You must try it.

Julie: Okay, I will. I feel like saying that I don't have the time, but I know that is not true. I find enough time to waste on other things and this is clearly important and something I am not doing enough of. This feels like a very important message.

All our messages are important, but this one involves you doing something and making a positive change to your life. Humans are resistant to change and that is the reason for you calling this message "important". It is a signal from your soul that you need to pay attention to this information and make a change in your life. This does not just apply to you: it is true of many people, and most of the people you know. You and they are walking round buildings and, in most cases, looking at things to buy which you do not need and which will not enhance your life. We are "suggesting" that you change that behaviour and do something much more fulfilling and more enjoyable, but most of all something that helps you to live your life in a more spiritual way and return to a "bliss state".

You can look from a window but the most benefit will be gained by interacting with it directly; by touching the soil and walking barefoot on the grass. Your energy is enhanced by it and you will feel "taller".

Julie: Taller?

Because your energy field will expand below your feet and above your head.

This does not just apply to countryside, of course. Walking by the sea or wherever is accessible to you, that can be counted as nature.

So clearly the message here is that we need to spend time in nature as often as we possibly can and, as discussed earlier, make sure that we move and stretch ourselves.

Moving Gracefully

If you are sitting reading this book and feeling anything but "graceful" I can truly sympathise! If you get up from the chair and your knees creak, you walk across the room and your hip hurts, and you need to find your glasses/stick etc. before you get much further, you might be wondering whether this section holds any relevance to you. But it is relevant because we can all move a little more gracefully if we think about it.

We have worked on energy moving freely around our home; we have decluttered unnecessary items and uplifted the space; and we have considered what we are putting into our bodies and the flow of energy between people, so it is obvious that we now need to give some more thought about how energy actually flows through our own bodies.

GUIDANCE FROM THE OTHER SIDE

In order to be truly graceful, we need to be able to move our bodies freely. To be able to turn, bend, balance and stretch in smooth lines, rather than in abrupt physical jerks. Not everyone is mobile, of course, but even if your movement is limited you can still move what you can move in a graceful fashion.

A definition of "graceful" (*Collins English Dictionary*, 2023):

"Characterised by elegance or beauty of form, manner, movement or speech; elegant."

You are beautiful whoever you are, you and your soul have beauty of form so it makes sense to align your movements in the same way. Your speech, too!

Being graceful is not a female characteristic, either. You do not have to be agile and built like a prima ballerina in order to move gracefully. You just need to learn to lengthen your movements, stretch your body where you can and think of a softer silhouette. It is more difficult to feel angry and tense if you are concentrating on moving gracefully.

As mentioned earlier, for those who can manage it, yoga is the perfect accompaniment to spiritual practice. It encourages graceful movement and leads you to think about the lines which you create with your body, and where the energy is going. There are many forms of yoga around with a variety of different names, so age and limited ability should not be a barrier if that is something you would enjoy doing. If you intend to join a class, it is worth researching which style is the most appropriate for you. When I was younger, my personal preference was for Ashtanga yoga because I felt that it gave me a better workout without going to the gym, but that is only one form and less appropriate for me now. If you have not tried yoga before, Hatha yoga is an excellent place to start, as that is designed to align mind, body and spirit through the practice of *asanas* (yoga postures), *pranayama* (yoga breathing) and other techniques designed to strengthen and purify the body and cultivate life force energy (Yoga Basics, 2007). "Chair yoga" and various other forms appear to be popular now and although they would not necessarily be approved of by purists, anything that gets people moving and helps energy to move around their body gets my vote. I sincerely hope that one day, yoga will be taught routinely in every school from Reception Classes upwards.

Regardless of how we achieve it, clearly the messages coming from the spirit world imply that moving gracefully and allowing energy to move freely around our body is beneficial for us.

The Ten Lessons

I have been very fortunate to have received a good deal of direct spirit communication. Besides Battrick, there is another spirit I call Victor who is keen to impart wisdom, but they are far from being the only ones. Whereas *Answers from the Other Side* was dictated systematically over a period of a few months, what has been included in this book is the result of many years' work. After the first book, the dictation did not follow what appeared at the time to be a logical format. I have had to work to see where it fits in and it is really only as I have got towards the end that some of that dictation makes sense. In May 2019 I was given the following ten lessons. I have left them in the order in which they were given to me. They do not necessarily follow the order in which they appear in the book, but they do relate to it:

- *Listen to your soul and it will guide you*
- *Move more gracefully in all things and stretch your body every day*
- *Respect the interconnectivity of nature; one action can affect a thousand things*
- *Walk in nature as often as you can, ideally every day*
- *Forgive and understand other people, however different they are from you and regardless of what they have done*
- *Listen to your dreams: there can be powerful guidance through sleep*

- *You need very little in terms of possessions: if you have too much or desire too much it will hold you back*
- *You are not alone, there are unseen powers assisting you and wishing you well*
- *You need to see beauty in all things*
- *You are "on holiday", even if you feel like a reluctant participant on a school trip; you must find joy in the process and have some fun before you return home*

In writing this book, it was made clear to me from the start that I had to actually live and experience everything I was saying. For the most part, this is what I have tried to do. We are not residing in the spirit world: we are here on earth, where the energy is much more dense. We are not perfect beings and we are here to learn as much as we can. Many of us came with long-forgotten agendas and maybe found ourselves in situations which felt cruel and unfathomable. Many of our attempts to be a better version of ourselves will be flawed, but the most important thing is that we pick ourselves up and keep on trying.

As more people attempt to live their lives in a more spiritual way, there will eventually be a tipping point and all our attempts will become much more fruitful. The world on earth will much more closely resemble the spirit world and we will return to a bliss state and will reunite.

Failing some of these spiritual challenges almost seems to be part of a bigger plan. I know what I should be doing to be fitter, healthier and more spiritual; that includes walking more in nature, but often I slide off the back of the metaphorical bus and then have to scramble to find my way back. Failing is what makes me human: I am not a machine and neither are you. I have a brain mind as well as a soul mind and they are not always in harmony. Rather than feel a failure, I have decided to see everything as an opportunity, because that is what I think is required here. Therefore, I cannot fail to learn as long as I keep trying. That is all that is asked of me. If it was easy and I got every lesson right first time and perfectly acted everything out until the day I died, I probably would not have learnt very much. So in summary, the only way I can fail is by not trying!

With every piece of information about the spirit world there is a temptation to think "Where and how does this fit?" I sometimes feel as though I have been given pieces of a jigsaw puzzle. I do not know how many pieces there should be, nor do I know the picture on the box. There is clearly much more to learn than I have been able to put here, but the more I learn about other-worldly things, the more there does appear to be some sort of plan. We have free will, without doubt, but it does appear as though we are born into places and families which will give us the best opportunity to progress our soul's development. If we appear to stray too far off course, our soul guidance mechanisms and the subconscious messages we sometimes receive in dreams appear to be designed to put us back on track. If this is the case, it does imply an intelligence of some sort from the highest to the lowest levels. I believe, too, that there may be strategic guardians which oversee the process; some communication I have received brings me to this conclusion.

Battrick goes on to say:
Living life in a more spiritual way is a subtle change in behaviour that is designed to intuit your soul or the souls of the people who undertake this. Everyone has a different agenda for living and this needs to be respected. There is no one way, or right way. Everything must be directed by the living soul and what it believes is right for its human at that time. The body is a vessel for the soul, but the body has its own energy, requirements and personal agenda relating to bodily functions and physical gratifications. The soul's agenda is a higher agenda and is more concerned with the overall good

of the planets, the source, and the soul's personal journey through all those things. Sometimes the body and soul clash. The physical bodily requirements can be very strong and can often overpower those of the soul.

Souls have requested that these bodily requirements are played down so that the soul's voice can be heard. The soul has, as part of its agenda, to protect the body and to keep it happy because happiness creates an energy that is beneficial for the soul. Unfortunately, the body believes that it knows what is needed for the body and follows unhealthy and unnecessary practices which satisfy immediate longings and cravings, but which are very bad for the body's development over time.

Even if you are a person who is strongly connected to your soul, you can still experience difficulty with these things. So it is necessary for you to put your soul first in all things and use your inner guidance to lead your actions for a healthier body and mind.

Everything is in place and ready for your needs. It is like having a book by your bedside that will solve all your problems, but not everyone chooses to read it. There are no hidden secrets – or if they are hidden then they are hidden in plain sight. They are there for the adoption. Notice that I do not say "there for the taking", as that implies that this will be easy and no effort is involved. That, of course, is not the case. If you are adopting something, it does imply effort and a change of behaviour which are of course necessary if you want your life to improve.

A more enlightened soul will listen to the guidance before the body needs to react at all. If something has a comfortable or pleasant taste and elicits some sort of chemical reaction in the brain then the body is very happy to let you carry on with the activity. This of course is the case with drugs, alcohol and certain types of food. An occasional indulgence to lift mood is not something that the soul wishes to deny the body (they are working in tandem and know each other well), but so many activities lead to the eventual destruction of the body's key vital signs, or at least a dulling of those signs over time. When this happens, it is so much more difficult for the soul to communicate. This happens a great deal and keeps people away from the sort of good, honest, reliable guidance that lets them lead a full and active life.

Julie: So how do we learn to recognise the soul's guidance before we get to this stage?
It is about listening. Everyone's soul talks to them in a slightly different way. There are different relationships. People talk about "gut feeling" and that is one way that a soul will talk to its vessel. Another is through dreams, or you may wake up one morning with some feeling that you believe needs to be acted upon. It can also be done through meditation and learning to trust what you might call your intuition. That is a reliable form of guidance, but only if the recipient has learned to listen correctly and has good hearing. The thing that needs to be practised regularly is learning to listen to the soul.

Julie: How can that be done?
It involves having quiet time and noting the thoughts which come to you. Dismiss any negative or unhealthy thoughts and note how to recognise those thoughts that are from your higher good. It is not easy to get this right – but the benefits are worth the effort.

Human souls are on a course – a track if you will – much like a train. They can decide to buy a ticket or not, to have some influence over the destination or not (provided the station does stop there), and then they can decide to break the journey, take another train to an interim destination, or they can decide to do some sightseeing and enjoy getting off at different stations along the way to convince themselves that they are on the right train/track. They have free will.

(Julie: I was told that I keep getting off the train just to check that I am in fact going in the right direction, that I do this constantly and that it does delay my journey. This made a lot of sense to me!)
Whatever you do, you learn a great deal along the way.

Without seeing the bigger picture, what you might consider a good choice in one respect might not be quite what the soul would have chosen for you. As always, your soul is your best friend. The problem with people incarnated on earth now is that many have not made their soul their best friend. This is their best guidance mechanism.

Julie: How will we know that we are following our soul guidance?

When the actions that you take have a familiarity to them. When coincidences work in your favour and when you might try to walk away but are brought back to where you need to be. Your body will experience better health and you will be happy with your choices, rather than fretting over them. When you take a step off the path you will enjoy the view, but will instinctively know when it is time to get back on the train. You will live in harmony as much as that is possible in an earthly existence. People will turn up at just the right time. Nothing will be forced – all will flow.

What you are doing now is trying to create peace on earth. A spiritual peace that is elusive for most people and only experienced for a few brief moments of earth time. The soul longs to create a spiritual existence on a physical plane, but it accepts that this is very difficult to achieve. This does not, however, stop it from trying. The soul has the power to influence and direct, but from the moment that humans are born, they stop listening. It takes practice and time, but this spiritual peace is a feeling that should resonate throughout your body. Your soul has the big picture and knows what is best for you.

The soul wants peace of mind and body!

The brain's feelings are learned behaviour or base instinct. You have not eaten for a while and you feel hunger. You stick your finger in a candle and *you feel pain. The soul uses feeling to guide you and the feeling it uses is one of love and peace. This is a complete and loving peace and it is important that everyone on this planet learns to recognise that.*

Trust is about acceptance and the willingness to perceive that life follows an orderly pattern. It is about a greater good and the knowledge that there is logic, pattern and order in that goodness. It is not always about fleeting desire or whim. It is about the soul's progress and its journey to earth being the main vessel to progress that journey.

Humans have free will. Without it they cannot learn. Some of the learning is designed to protect the body – the vessel of the soul and not connected to the soul's development. There are two intelligences and one is body-related – the other is soul related. The body has desires and to a large extent these will be satisfied if they do not affect the journey of the soul. The body and soul both influence the brain and the brain makes decisions which are sometimes body-related and at other times soul-related. In an ideal world (one you do not always live in, nor anyone else on earth) the two elements work in harmony. You know when the two are working together, as everything flows and people experience coincidences which lead them in a certain direction. When the brain devises paths to follow which are not soul-related then it feels like swimming against the tide. You might get there in the end, but the effort does not justify the journey and you realise that there would have been an easier route which would have taken you to a more desirous (soul-related) outcome.

Julie: So how can we recognise body desire, as opposed to soul desire?

When it is in tune with the body, the soul knows what the body needs not only to survive but to work to its optimum level. Then the soul will work with the body and help keep the vessel in the best working order possible so that it can help to fulfil the soul's mission on earth. When not in tune, body and soul can appear to work for opposing forces and this can result in a feeling of running around in circles and becoming more tired and deflated. If this continues for long enough, that can result in illness.

The mission of each soul can be extremely complex and the soul may wish to experience situations which the body does not feel are desirous for its overall health. These might be experiences which lead to a deterioration of its mental health or pain and illness in the body which the soul knows further its learning and cannot be avoided. Although the soul has a desire to work with the body to fulfil its mission, it knows that sometimes some pain, discomfort, anxiety or depression are necessary in order to lead to a more desirous state in the future.

Humans have expectations and not all those expectations will be met in this life. This does not imply a failure in this life. Quite the opposite: it can represent great learning and triumph.

In all dark corners there is learning and greater understanding. All of this helps to progress the soul and take it to its next level. It is not appropriate to give up and want to return home. The seemingly less desirous life must be lived. Not all learning happens at once. It is not enough to say – I know what this disability feels like now, so beam me up and take me home – it is done. The reality to the soul is that it is far from done. It is not over until the soul decides to return home. This should be a soul decision and not a body brain decision. If the soul does not experience full learning, then it will set up a situation to ensure that the learning is experienced at another time. That might be in another life or even in a soul state. It depends on what learning has been lost.

Julie: How can we on earth assist the soul with its learning so that the process is as painless as possible?

Bringing body and soul together is what needs to happen. This is done through silent meditation and what is now described on your planet as "mindfulness". The more the body and soul communicate, the greater chance there is of the two working in harmony. Not all pain and suffering can be avoided, let us be very clear about this: you have an expression called "groundhog day" and this can be avoided if body and soul work in harmony. Many people repeat the same actions and wonder why they get the same results. The soul and spiritual forces may be shouting at the body vessel to take different action and yet this is ignored. The body can only see its most desirous outcome in the short term and follows that.

The task is to relax and detach from any preconceived outcomes about what would be the most desirable state. Any voices that are heard at this point should be acknowledged but ignored. The soul will communicate when it is ready and not before. There will be no voice in your ear giving precise instructions about what to do. It will be an internal "knowing", which eventually is felt in the pit of the stomach, that becomes apparent when body and soul are aligned. This could take weeks, months or years. This is not a quick-fix technique. It is about harmony.

I wish to say that however dark the days may appear to some, there is never any point, not even for a fleeting second, when they are on their own. Besides the people attempting to support them in this life, there is a very wide circle of souls supporting them in the afterlife. They are wishing them well and offering practical help that supports the help being given in the physical. To make the most of those unseen forces, they need to work at being more relaxed and calmer. They are not alone. Their soul knows exactly what has to happen and they do not need to think about it, force it, try and make it go down a different route – they just need to foster calm relaxed detachment and attempt to let things wash over them until harmony is returned. It is a very difficult thing to do because it requires someone to "let go", and many anxiety conditions come about because people want to control everything around them. That is not realistic. If every soul tried to control everything around them there would be constant conflict. Harmony is about balance and that must be left to forces which can see the bigger picture.

Detachment requires trust. You cannot detach from an outcome unless you trust that the outcome will be for the greater good. You are unlikely to *be able to see how that greater good plays out, and especially how that will impact on your individual situation, so you must trust that the greater good will result in the best possible outcome for your soul and for the souls around you.*

This concludes the directly-channelled material in this book. In *Answers from the Other Side* (2022), most of the book is channelled directly from Battrick because in order to get those answers it was necessary to talk to someone who had experienced death and who was residing on the other side of life. This book is about how we live as incarnated souls on earth, and to do that requires a combination of earthly and spiritual experience.

We Are All Work In Progress

Something that has been made very clear to me whilst writing this book is that I not only needed to fully experience everything I was writing about but that that a spiritual life must be "discovered".

This book has taken many years to write and I would be the first to admit that I am still "work in progress". I have been as honest as I can about where I am on my journey. Like everyone else I start things, but it may be a while before they become wholly integrated into my life. Life "stuff" has a habit of getting in the way and sending me off-course, just as it no doubt does for everyone else. As I said earlier, the only way I can fail is by not trying at all.

From what I understand, the spirit world has a vested interest in us waking up, knowing and experiencing the fact that our physical bodies are just vessels for our soul. It appears to help our soul development if we come to this realisation whilst in the physical body, rather than waiting until we pass over. The implication is that we are more likely to develop the soul if we actually know and accept that it is there.

According to Silver Birch, the spirit channelled by Maurice Barbanell (1986), we are incarnated on earth in order to experience polar extremes which are not possible in the spirit world. It is only by experiencing those extremes that we can fully learn. Although our soul lessons continue after death, it seems there is not the opportunity to experience polar opposites to the same extent. This is understandable if the spirit world is a place of love and higher vibrational frequencies. You can only fully appreciate what it is like to be free from pain, whether physical or emotional, if you have actually experienced it. You certainly cannot experience physical pain in the spirit world because there is no physical, and so we start to get an idea about why we might be here. This has to be true for joy and happiness: how can we know true joy or that bliss state if we have not experienced the opposite at some point in our soul's development?

I do believe that we have a choice as to whether we reincarnate either on this planet or any other and presumably those decisions are made on the basis of what we have left to experience. If we can reach the bliss state that Battrick talks about then we can stop this cycle of birth, death and rebirth, and learn what was intended while we are here.

According to what was channelled to me for *Answers from the Other Side*, the learning we do is eventually returned to our source and it is this which allows the source to expand. That being the case, it is possible to attempt to understand that the spirit world needs us to do what we set out to do before birth and fulfil our obligations. This appears to be why it is so important that we learn our lessons now.

The fact that you are reading this means that you are at least contemplating how your soul may progress. You can read this book for yourself and decide which lessons, if any, apply to you. I had to go on the same journey of discovery to write this book as someone who reads it. There are no mistakes, just learning. I am still working on many of the things mentioned here, but at least my eyes are open to that soul connection and the guidance that can be obtained by "going within".

So if the only way we can fail is by not trying, what do we have to lose?

There is learning, whether we make that soul connection or not. Be kind to yourself. Give yourself time and think about what is truly important to you and see how those aims feel to you. By "being spiritual" you are raising your vibrational frequency and your awareness. You cannot fail.

Using Our Power To Help and Heal Others
It is my firm belief that one of the most productive things we can do to help others, and by association ourselves, is to send out healing. This is a lot less complicated than it sounds and is all about the clear and loving intention to help others heal themselves.

By connecting to our soul body, all the healer has to do is to put in place a clear intention to heal. I honestly don't think it matters what sort of technique is adopted. I was trained in Reiki and that included something called an "attunement", which some believe made it easier to be a healing channel, but intention appears to be the most important factor. The healing goes where it is needed. That does not mean that we should always expect a miracle cure: far from it. Healing can take many forms and may just promote better understanding and acceptance, if that is what is needed. The person being healed does not have to believe in alternative healing, or even know that even healing is taking place, although at soul level I ask permission to send healing. And of course, at no point should anyone ever refuse traditional medical intervention over any sort of spiritual healing. Healers supplement; they do not replace. If a miracle should happen (and I believe they can), that is between the subject of the healing and the spirit world. The actual "healer" had very little to do with in.

If you are interested in healing, there are many courses or institutions which you can go to if you would like to find out more. They should have a very strict code of practice about what is acceptable, encourage official registration and insurance from an independent body, and be well respected and reviewed. As with everything, some practitioners and teachers are better than others, so it is essential that you do your research, whether you want to receive healing or give it. There is something to be said for a personal recommendation from someone you trust.

With permission, healing is available for everyone, it does not discriminate and it should not require someone to part with excessive sums of money in order to receive it (some of the best healers I know charge nominal rates). It is not going to run out, it is not limited to a select number of people and it can be just as powerful for thousands as it can be for one.

Remote Healing

There is of course no requirement to do any formal training if you just want to send healing thoughts to another human being. We can all do that and it can be no less powerful than if it is coming from a registered healer.

Prayer could be described as a form of remote healing. If enough people get together to affect a particular healing change then that is intention. To be effective, a channel needs to be put in place, but this can be done in many different ways. It can be done by prayer, for example, or just by asking the spirit world for assistance.

In remote healing, the healer quietly sets the intention to help one or several people. Healing can be accepted or rejected at spirit soul level by the subject to be healed, so it is not necessary to ask permission from a living person as such for remote healing. Sometimes their spirit is buried in pain and discomfort. It is not always necessary or possible to ask first when doing healing from a remote location, any more than we might ask someone if we can pray for them.

Your intention acts as a bridge between the two worlds, a direct line can be established and the healing becomes effective. It doesn't matter what method is used, the simpler the better, so that the subject receives healing sooner rather than later.

As we have seen with Control Dramas, energy passes between people and giving positive healing energy to another human being will not deplete you if you are just sending healing thoughts. In fact, if you do this regularly you will be raising your energy vibration and, as we know, like attracts like, so we can also benefit from the healing we send out.

Just imagine a world where this was commonplace. Where no jealousy exists, where no one judges anyone, but where everyone lives with the intention to uplift absolutely everyone they meet. Unfortunately that seems a long way off, but the (only) way we can effect this sort of change is to be the change we want to see. Then the world will change, one soul at a time.

A Strategy For Moving Forward
There is a lot to take in here and it can become overwhelming without developing a strategy for moving forward. The most important thing is to find or maintain that soul connection and then analyse your life and decide what you want or do not want in it in future.

Not everyone will feel comfortable writing in a journal, but however you do it thinking about what you are grateful to have in your life now is a good place to start. We often fail to appreciate some of the simple things which make us happy.

If you can use some of the techniques suggested to refine a vision for your future self, all well and good. Much depends on where you are currently in life. If you are just starting out then the vision could look very different to one envisaged when you are thinking about giving up work altogether. It really doesn't matter. Whatever age we are in this life, our soul is eternal. There is no need for us to conform to age-related stereotypes, or to feel as though the things we would like to do are on ships which have already sailed. When I was thinking about doing something and wondering if it was a good idea, someone told me, "The spirit world does not care how old you are!" Of course! Why would they? The soul does not age, only the physical body. Working for the spirit world does not have a recommended retirement age. So why should anything else we want to do? The point about writing down your vision in detail is that it might alert you to more ways in which it could be achieved. We must factor in practicality, clearly, but it doesn't have to squash every idea we have. There may not be a solution today, but if we are aligned to what our soul wants for us then something may show up tomorrow that makes some of those dreams more of a reality. So take time writing your vision, and keep revisiting it. You never know where it may take you!

If you have a lifetime of possessions and you love them all, do not feel pressured into getting rid of things immediately. As a strategy, you might just decide to apply the suggestions to the room you spend most of your time in. On the other hand, you may see decluttering as just what you need at the moment. Whatever approach you adopt, take the time to write down what you are going to do. The mere fact of committing it to paper increases the commitment.

You may decide that you need to work a little bit more on honouring your body as a vehicle for your soul by being more careful about what you eat/drink and ensuring that you move gracefully so that energy can move freely around your body. Whatever changes you feel are necessary to bring you greater happiness, these can be greatly encouraged by committing them to paper. There is a Strategy template for this purpose at the end of the Resources section which I hope you will find helpful.

The spirit world is there to help us, so asking for strength and resolve to deal with our personal issues is not only acceptable but a very good idea. Clearly, we are not in this alone. By taking the necessary steps and then asking for support, we reinforce our efforts.

Thank you for getting this far and reading what I have to say. This book has been written with the sole objective of trying to help people navigate their way through some of life's challenges by benefiting from the soul guidance on offer. It is hoped that the exercises which follow will assist you on that journey. Thank you.

GUIDANCE FROM THE OTHER SIDE

Chapter 5 Summary: Stepping Into Your True Power

- It is important to walk in nature at every opportunity. It enlightens your soul, enhances your spiritual connection and helps to connect you to the wider universe

- Allow energy to flow freely around your body by moving more gracefully. If you can, make yoga a part of your life

- Remember the ten lessons:
    1. Listen to your soul and it will guide you
    2. Move more gracefully in all things and stretch your body every day
    3. Respect the interconnectivity of nature: one action can affect a thousand things
    4. Walk in nature as often as you can, ideally every day
    5. Forgive and understand other people, however different they are from you and regardless of what they have done
    6. Listen to your dreams: there can be powerful guidance through sleep
    7. You need very little in terms of possessions; if you have too much or desire too much it will hold you back
    8. You are not alone, there are unseen powers assisting you and wishing you well
    9. You need to see beauty in all things
    10. You are "on holiday", even if you feel like a reluctant participant on a school trip; you must find joy in the process and have some fun before you return home

- We are all work in progress, every one of us. We are here to learn and that learning continues when we pass to the spirit world

GUIDANCE FROM THE OTHER SIDE

- Send positive energy and healing thoughts to anyone who needs them

- Develop your own personal strategy to make the most of the suggestions contained in this book

GUIDANCE FROM THE OTHER SIDE

PRACTICE RESOURCES
A: Meditation To Connect To Your Soul Self

This is a meditation to give you the opportunity to start to notice your own sense of self. It requires you to use your imagination as best you can, but there are no hard and fast rules and it can be adapted to suit. Take your time. It will be easier to do this on some occasions than others. You can play music if it helps, as long as that music doesn't distract you or send you to sleep. I believe that in an ideal world it helps to meditate at a set time each day. This isn't always possible, but it helps if you can manage it.

As you sit in this meditation, aim to get a little bit further each time. It is far better to concentrate on carefully imagining the light enveloping you and feeling fully protected by it than it is to rush ahead.

- Find a quiet place to sit where you hope you will not be interrupted for a while
- Put your feet flat on the floor and place your upturned palms comfortably on your lap
- Close your eyes and just allow yourself to become aware of your breathing
- For a moment or two, just notice the rise and fall of your breath
- At this point some people like to imagine their feet growing roots and sending those roots into the earth
- Start by imagining a small flame starting to flicker in the centre of your being
- Imagine the flame gradually getting stronger and stronger, brighter and brighter
- When you are ready, try to imagine the flame growing into a white light forming in the centre of your body – this is your inner guiding light
- Watch that light getting stronger and brighter
- Focus on it getting larger and spreading out beyond your physical body by up to 30 cm or so, or as far as you can manage

GUIDANCE FROM THE OTHER SIDE

Take as long as you like. If any stray thoughts come into your head during this time, just briefly acknowledge them and then watch them float away.

- *Imagine that the light covers your whole body – not just around your torso and head: aim for it to expand some distance from your feet as well*
- *You should be able to feel as though you are protected by a clear white light that becomes an egg-shaped bubble as it covers your whole body*
- *On the outer rim of this egg-shaped bubble of light is a special thin shell-like filter that protects you*
- *It will only let in the purest energy of the highest order; it will also let you send your love and empathy out to all who need it*
- *Sit within this light-filled bubble for a while and notice how it feels*

This is the time to become acquainted with the feeling of "self" inherent in the bubble of light. Do you notice anything about the energy? How does it feel to you? Does the energy feel light and energising? Does it feel soft and loving? It helps if you just sit with the feeling, rather than sitting expecting anything in particular to happen.

- *The aim now is to get a sense of your self soul within the light-filled bubble*
- *Your soul is pure light-filled energy and is enlightened in the true sense of the word*
- *Can you become aware of your deep consciousness within the bubble?*
- *Are there any helpful images which come to mind as you sit there?*
- *Regardless, rest in this spot and enjoy the feeling*
- *You are starting to become acquainted with your own soul*
- *Slowly come out of the meditation when you are ready*
- *Open your eyes and gently stand up and stamp your feet*

GUIDANCE FROM THE OTHER SIDE

As you come out of the meditation, you can decide to keep the light-filled bubble with you. If you are living or working with negative people, retaining the feeling of the bubble can be helpful when going about your day. The special filter that is in place will protect you from the negativity dispensed by others and will help you to stay positive and happy.

B: Journaling Exercise
Writing down your thoughts, rather than just mulling them over in your head, is a key step in understanding yourself and your motivations. My personal preference is to write things down in a beautiful notebook that has been bought for the purpose. The more attractive it is, the more magical it will feel. There is something very special about picking up your best pen and starting a new page in a brand-new notebook: it speaks of greater understanding and new beginnings. It isn't a problem if you are more comfortable using a laptop, rather than writing things by hand, but please be aware that technology can be as distracting as it is useful. If you are journaling whilst in a state of semi-meditation, writing by hand, it might be easier to retain the connection, but this is all about you and your personal connection with your soul, so whatever you feel most comfortable with is just fine.

You can choose to journal every day at the same time, such as first thing in the morning or last thing at night, or you can just pick up your journal when you feel you have something to record, a decision to make or some feelings to sort out.

Different methods:
1. Start by asking a question (write it at the top of the page) and see if you sense an answer to your question.
2. Write freely about your feelings – whether you feel happy or sad, uncertain or confused. Don't wait for a solution, just write, but as different viewpoints come into your head record those as well.

3. You can read it like a diary inasmuch as you write in it every day, but don't spend too long writing factual information about where you have been or what you have done. This is about the spiritual rather than the physical, about feelings and emotions rather than actual events.
4. Making decisions: write your options at the top of the page and record the pros and cons of each action – "feeling into" each one.

Analysis
The journal will work best if you re-read what you have written and use it to try to understand other points of view and your own actions. For example, if you write in your journal that work colleague X always seems to undermine your authority, go back and read exactly what they said and how you reacted to their comments. Try to understand what might make them act in this way and what might have prompted them to do that. It may not be easy to identify others' motivations initially, but see if a pattern emerges and ask yourself if you do need more experience in certain areas or whether their original comments could have been interpreted in another way.

There can be misunderstandings within families and we often play out the same family dramas (please refer to the section on Control Dramas in Chapter 4 for further information). If the same behaviour is repeating itself at regular intervals, then there is a case for analysing what is actually happening and trying to pave a way to better understanding. A journal is the perfect place to do this. For example, a son who returning home from university has become used to a certain amount of freedom and, although he may be benefitting from all the financial benefits of returning home, could be feeling "unreasonably" confined by restrictions which were taken for granted before he left. On the other hand, you have a parent who has been used to having their home just as they wanted it for the last three or four years and now feels obliged to take up a parental role that they had comfortably left behind. Add in the son who gets up late because he is starting to get depressed and cannot find a job, plus a sink full of unwashed plates, and there's a potential for major disharmony. Far better for both parties to make a serious attempt to understand where the other person is coming from and find a place where the dialogue can begin. It is worth playing out some of the scenarios in your journal to try and understand where the other person is coming from before you approach them.

One final thought about journaling: they are for your eyes only. They represent you working through your various issues and coming to terms with how and why things need to change. Emotions can be raw and sometimes not truly representative of how you truly feel, especially when they are first expressed, so they are best kept in a secure place while you work things out.

C: Gratitude Exercise

Somewhere in your journal, or even in a separate journal, there should be a section devoted to gratitude. It is only by regularly giving thanks for what we already have that we can be truly happy.

When the world weighs heavily on our soul it can be difficult to give thanks when we are feeling so low. The tendency is to think about what we don't have, rather than what we do. At such times, think small:

I am grateful for the bed that I sleep in today
I am grateful for the roof over my head today
I am grateful for the food that I have to eat today.

There are times in our lives when it is far too difficult and painful to think beyond today. Today can feel as though that is all we have and we are far too fearful to think about tomorrow. At these times it is more important than ever to appreciate what we have. Look hard and list everything that you value, however small it may be. Read the list tomorrow, and the day after, and add to it as you think of more things to be grateful for.

When we are in a better position, it is much easier to add to the list; as we do so, we can feel the joy that all those precious things give to us:

I am grateful for my wonderful children
I am grateful for my beautiful new bicycle
I am grateful for my adoring cat…

It is all too easy to focus on the negative and not give thanks for all the wonderful gifts which we have in our lives. Your gratitude list is something to cherish, read often and add to.

D: Happy Balance Wheel

Please refer to Chapter 2 when doing this exercise, as the purpose is to provide you with a visual representation of the overall balance or "happy balance" that you have in your life. At the end of the exercise, you should have a good idea of the areas where you need to focus more of your attention.

To create a happy balance wheel, take a piece of paper and draw a large circle on it. Divide that circle into (as suggested) eight sections, as if you were dividing up a cake. Within each section, draw a faint line with ten sections on it, as below. The point nearest the centre of the circle is 1 and the point on the edge is 10.

GUIDANCE FROM THE OTHER SIDE

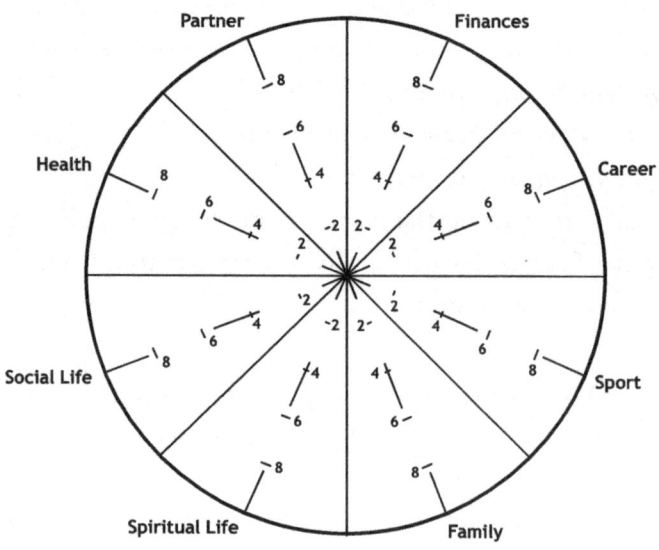

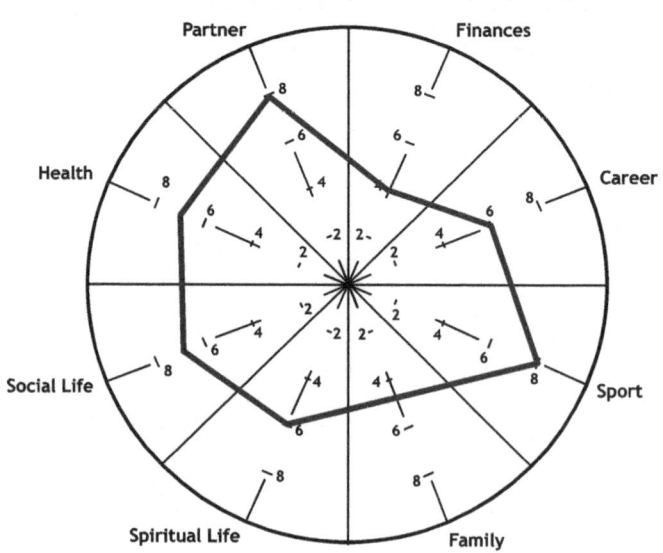

GUIDANCE FROM THE OTHER SIDE

As discussed in Chapter 2, decide on ideally no more than eight areas of your life where you need to focus your attention. Typical segments might be partner; children; other family; friends; your career; your mental and physical health; your passion (music, football, art); your spiritual connection; and your finances (for example). The sections should represent things which you care about and want to spend time on. If you cannot think of eight then that is fine. Just complete as many as are appropriate to you.

When you have a name for each segment, place a cross on the lines 1-10 (1 = low, 10 = high) within each section, based on how happy and fulfilled you currently feel in each area. Then join the crosses together. You then end up with something that may look nothing like a circle. Where the line dips inwards is an indication of where you may need to make some changes.

It is much easier to feel happy and fulfilled if you have found a good balance and all the things that are important to you are receiving enough of your attention. To redress any imbalance, the next stage is to make a list of a maximum of three things which you can do to find that happy balance, and maybe up to three things which you need to stop doing. For example, you may feel that you have neglected playing sport and that you need to find a new club to play for. You may have to acknowledge that you spend too long on your phone and need to limit that time to a fixed number of hours per day so that you have time to get back into sport and improve your physical health. This is just a useful tool to help you to think through everything that is important to you.

Put a date on your diagram and lists and then repeat the exercise in three or six months' time. By that time you should hopefully have a visual representation of how you have regained the balance in some areas of your life.

E: Recording Your Vision

It is not enough just to think about what you want. You need to write down your hopes and aspirations for yourself in some detail and word them very carefully.

Why write them down?
1. It makes you think about the language you are using and it will encourage you to write your wishes in the present tense, as though your dreams have already manifested.
2. You are making a form of contract with yourself, so you need to be clear about what it says.
3. You can read your vision to yourself at regular intervals and make sure that it is still what you want.
4. You can look back at a later date and see how your dreams have manifested for you.
5. If you feel as though nothing has changed, ask yourself if that vision that you have needs further analysis. Are these things really best for you? If you decide that they are, then sit down and think about some practical steps which you can take to make those things a reality.

Even if you decide to use electronic means to record your vision for yourself, make sure that you keep a copy close by so that you can re-read the words on a regular basis. Repeat the words out loud, if possible, as often as you can. Remember, this is your contract with yourself, so you do not need to get anyone else involved unless you really want to. Even the most well-meaning friends and family can put you off by laughing at you for daring to think that you can become more than you already are. You do not need to prove anything to anyone; your dreams are your dreams and you have every right to have them. Just because no one else in your family has done it doesn't mean that you cannot be the first. Often, family just wants to avoid the possibility of your being disappointed if you cannot achieve your goals. But which is worse? Having a dream and maybe not achieving everything that you had hoped for, but knowing that you got close and gave it your best shot, or not daring to dream and not achieving what you hope for yourself?

It may help you to get a large piece of paper, or sit at a laptop, and create five columns. Then select five headings or categories. The ones shown below are just suggestions. Chapter 2 goes into more detail about the sort of things you need to consider, so if it has been a while since you have read Chapter 2 it would be a good idea to go back and review it.

Relationships	Career/Job	Family	Finances	Social Activity

You can of course choose whatever headings you wish. Take one category at a time and describe your "ideal" under each heading. It is essential that you write in the present tense and as you write (or create) your ideal: really feel it. Imagine that you are describing your life as it is now. The universe works on how everything feels to you, so whether it has happened in the physical or is in your imagination is of no consequence. The objective is to align your conscious energy with what you wish to create for yourself.

It is important not to focus or write anything that indicates that something is missing in your life, so avoid words such as I "want" more time/more money/to move/love. The universe will oblige and leave you "wanting", so write as though you have time to spend with your loved ones and enjoy holidays and days out in the countryside, or whatever your vision is.

You can work on your vision over time so as to get it as you want it. You may be very surprised at how quickly some things appear.

If you are finding it difficult to work out what you actually want and what your vision for yourself should be, answering these questions might help you:

1. Where do I want to live? In what part of the world?
2. Do I want to live in a city? A town/village? Countryside, or by the sea?
3. What sort of work do I want to do?
4. How important is it that I work in something very sociable, where I am working with people every day? Or do I want to work in a more solitary environment – possibly on my own at home?
5. Which is the most important to me: a high salary, or a sense of achievement, or the fact that I am helping others? Or it is essential that I achieve all these things?
6. Do I want/can I cope with work stress in my life to achieve my aim? Or do I want stress levels to be low and not to think about work when I leave it?
7. Could I work for myself, or do I need the security of paid work?
8. Do I have to consider any other significant people when I am thinking about my future? What are their hopes and aspirations?
9. How important are money and status to me?
10. Are there other things outside work that I want to achieve? To be a sportsperson, charity worker, artist, etc.?
11. Do I wish to have a family and how will this impact on any of my decisions?
12. Do I need to incorporate a lot of change into my life because I easily get bored, or am I happy to settle down and work somewhere for a long time?

13. If I would rather not work at all, what would I like in place in my life to make that possible, and what would I spend my time doing if I did not have a traditional work commitment?
14. What do I want to be able to say about myself when I get towards the end of my life?
15. Is there anything in my heart that I believe I am here to do?

F: Self-Sabotage Exercise

From the moment we were born into this life we pick up signals from everyone and everything around us about how the world works. Unfortunately, some of those signals are faulty and not serving in our best interest. Consequently, we have some preconceived ideas about how the world works and sometimes those ideas lurk beneath the surface of our consciousness and trip us up.

When we look at successful people, we may be inclined to think that they had to display a certain amount of selfishness and single-mindedness to get where they are. We may not identify with the traits of selfishness and single-mindedness in ourselves and we may equate being successful with being unkind, or not putting our families first. If you think of yourself as a spiritual person – and I certainly do – then being selfish is not something I wish to identify with. On the other hand, we may not wish to shine too brightly in case other people feel jealous of us and wish us anything less than the best. Maybe we are concerned that we will lose some of our friends if we start to achieve our dreams? This might be true of a struggling artist who feels that they are "selling out" if someone wants to give them a lot of money for their work. Or it could be that we are afraid that being successful will move us into a social circle where we might feel uncomfortable. Whatever the reasons, these ideas can undermine what we are trying to achieve and give us the excuses not to push ahead. What if I am not good enough? What if my friends hate me because I am more successful than them? In the end, it can just be down to fear!

So, what can we do? Well, we need to unpick every preconceived idea about what achieving our dreams might involve and learn to come to peace with them.

Take one dream that you are struggling with and go into your light-filled bubble. Ask if you are self-sabotaging your dreams and ask whether you have any preconceived ideas which are not serving you well. Be prepared to learn. Be prepared to examine your deepest thoughts and be prepared to change your thinking.

I have certainly suffered from self-sabotaging in the past and analysing those blockages has certainly helped me.

I would start by asking myself a series of questions: "What is stopping me from achieving X?" "What do I really think about people who have achieved X?" "Will I have to adopt qualities I do not like to achieve X?" "Will people be jealous of me?" "Will I lose my friends?" By asking yourself each relevant question, one by one, you start to build up a picture about what might be holding you back. Some of your concerns will be valid, but many will not. Even when there are valid concerns, you can ask your higher soul self, whilst in a meditative state, how you can mitigate some of the issues which may be holding you back.

You can be whoever you want, including the kindest, softest, most loving person, and still achieve your goals. Look out for where you might be sabotaging your dreams and be prepared to analyse your thinking.

GUIDANCE FROM THE OTHER SIDE

G: Dream Template

You may find it helpful to record your dreams using a template.

Dream date:
Description of dream
Was there a message?
How does it relate to what has been going on recently in my life?
Any clearer later on? (date)

GUIDANCE FROM THE OTHER SIDE

I: Strategy Template

This is your contract template with yourself. If there are any issues which you would like to work on or explore further, you can record them here:

Question	Y/N	Issue	Action
1. Do I feel that I have established a strong soul connection?			
2. Have I established a clear vision for my future self?			
3. Have I worked out where I need to focus my attention?			
4. Am I happy with the sacred space that I have created for myself and my home?			
5. Do I feel writing my thoughts and feelings in a journal will be helpful for me?			
6. Is procrastination a problem for me, and if so, do I feel better able to use time slots to deal with it?			
7. Do I feel more able to notice the coincidences and synchronicity, and take more notice of my dreams?			
8. Have I been able to recognise Control Drama within my own family and friendship groups?			
9. Do I move my body sufficiently and gracefully to provide the best possible vessel for my soul?			
10. Do I walk in nature enough to allow myself to benefit from everything it has to offer?			
11. Do I feel more in control of my own happiness?			
12. Am I able to uplift others with kind words, actions and healing energy?			

A SINCERE "THANK YOU"

Thank you so much for buying this book, or for downloading an electronic copy.

With millions of books available to you, I am most grateful that you decided on this one and sincerely trust that it is everything you hoped it would be.

If you have found that these words have meaning for you, may I ask you to be brave and discuss some of these concepts with anyone you think they may help? Lots of people are struggling at the moment and the world is a confusing and sometimes frightening place for many. Other worldly topics are often subjected to ridicule and that prevents many people from sharing what they know to be true. Until we attain that tipping point of souls who recognise that they are spirit energy first and physical matter second, very little will change.

Remember, this life is not all there is and we can change the world, one soul at a time.

Thank you.

Julie

REFERENCES

Burgin T (2007) Hatha Yoga: Definition, History & Benefits, Yoga Basics [online] available from https://www.yogabasics.com/learn/hatha-yoga-the-physical-path

Chase S (nd) Goodreads Quotes [online] available from https://www.goodreads.com/author/quotes/1051789.Stuart_Chase [25 August 2023]

Psychic News (2003) Developing your mind body and spirit [online] available from http://about.psychicnews.org.uk [25 August 2023]

Redfield J. (1994) *The Celestine Prophecy: An Adventure.* Bantam Books

Redfield J. (1997) *The Celestine Vision.* Bantam Books

Watts C., Conkin J. (nd) Adobe.com: Use Kirlian Photography to Create High-voltage photo images [online], available from https://www.adobe.com/uk/creativecloud/photography/discover/kirlian-photography.html> [25 August 2023]

Wells, David (2008) *Real People, Real Past Lives.* Hay House

BIBLIOGRAPHY

The Spiritual Truth Foundation (2009) Silver Birch Series, Compiler Ortzen T. *The Seed of Truth*. Booksprint.

The Spiritual Truth Foundation (2009) Silver Birch Series, Compiler Ortzen T. *The Spirit Speak*. Booksprint.

The Spiritual Truth Foundation (2012) Silver Birch Series, Editor Ortzen T. *A Voice in the Wilderness*. Booksprint.

The Spiritual Truth Foundation (2009) Silver Birch Series, Editor Naylor W. *Silver Birth Anthology*. Booksprint.

The Spiritual Truth Foundation (2013) Silver Birch Series, Editor Ortzen T. *Silver Birch Companion*. Booksprint.

GUIDANCE FROM THE OTHER SIDE

GUIDANCE FROM THE OTHER SIDE